TOUR DE FRANCE 2002

 The Official Guide

Foreword
Jean-Marie Leblanc
Tour de France race director

Texts
Jacques Augendre

Captions and stage summaries
Denis Descamps

Photographers
Bruno Bade, Ingrid Hoffmann & Jean-Christophe Moreau

Translation
Theresa O'Neill & Denis Descamps

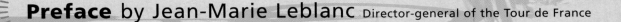
The Road to the Centennial Tour

As we turn the page on this 2002 Tour de France, I'm torn between two subjects that both bring me a great deal of satisfaction.

The first is the race itself and how it was run: the daily attitude of the riders, their competitive yet generous nature; the panache of some, starting with Laurent Jalabert, but also including Santiago Botero, Robbie McEwen, Michaël Boogerd, and Richard Virenque; and, of course, the unmatched performance of the winner, Lance Armstrong.

To the magnificence of the race must be added the sporting atmosphere in which it took place, a much calmer one than we have known for the last four years. It was implicitly acknowledged by all members of the caravan—including the press—that every effort should be taken by all of the parties involved to ensure that this edition of the Tour would be preserved from the demons haunting it since 1998.

Over the course of the three weeks of the Tour, we took great pleasure in following a lively and captivating competition while, paradoxically, we virtually knew the name of the winner before the race started. This is the magic of the Tour, when the setting is right, the scenario well structured, and the actors are well chosen.

Unfortunately, we had to be reminded yet again, through the seemingly stupid, extravagant, and reprehensible behavior of Mrs. Edita Rumsas on the final day of the race, that the anti-doping battle will be a long and inexhaustible one. We hold out hope that the World Anti-Doping Agency will soon help in this crusade with all its moral power, financial means, and prescribed clarity.

But for a moment let us forget this side of the sport, which still obsesses us, to look at another, infinitely more fortifying and hopeful, aspect of cycling. I simply want to talk about you, the spectators, television viewers, and the fans—the people of the Tour de France. Whether French or from abroad, people of all ages and social origins, male and female, you all came together to give a warm welcome to the Tour and its riders. You did it every day and it was a great success. Those who have been around the Tour for a long time, or around other sports—as I have been—have never before seen such crowds and felt such emotion.

This great celebration started from the first stage in Luxembourg, where our hosts in the Grand Duchy noted that the Tour attracted more spectators than

there were inhabitants, with many in attendance from Germany, Belgium, the Netherlands, and France, to name just a few of the countries represented. The jubilation reached new heights as the Tour passed through Germany, where a gigantic party was held, with banners, flags, music, costumes, and dancing, prepared for by the Saar people to welcome an event that they had waited nearly ten years for, and yet local hero Jan Ullrich did not participate in the 2002 Tour!

The Champagne region (where pride, inventiveness, and happiness were rampant) and Brittany lived up to their reputations as "cycling-mad regions," and we soon found ourselves in Picardy, Normandy (hats off to St. Martin-de-Landelles, the hometown of official Tour speaker Daniel Mangeas), and then the Pyrénées (with its Basque flags and the daily parade of campers that are now part of the Tour's daily set up).

In the meantime, French hero Laurent Jalabert had announced his impending retirement, and there was a resulting tidal wave of sympathy banners for him. Our friend Jacques Augendre writes about all the good things this magnificent rider has brought to the French people, who loved him all the more as they discovered the extent of his charm a little late.

Then there were the literally overheated regions of Languedoc and Provence, even more inflamed by the exploits of Richard Virenque on the arid slopes of Mont Ventoux. A jubilant atmosphere, with a few extremes, of course (the insults shouted at Lance Armstrong, thankfully without consequences), but with a passion that lifted the Tour de France to new heights in terms of an almost cathartic fusion between an event and its public.

And we weren't let down by the Alps, which provided us with magnificent scenery and an action-packed competition, again complemented by the French television team of Frédéric Chevit and Jean-Maurice Ooghe, whose work, as you may have seen, often verged on masterpieces.

Lest you think that I am giving way to euphoria or intoxicated by the nice weather that was with us all the way, the numerous verbal and written testimonies received three days after the finish in Paris, tell me that I am not the only one. Our partners, along with the local town councils, shared this passion. The Galibier, the Madeleine, La Plagne, and the Colombière were festive climbs; the time trial between Régnié-Durette and Mâcon was perfect; and I pay tribute to my friends Jean-François Pescheux and Jean-Louis Pagès, who so competently selected the itineraries, and the start and finish sites. Theirs was a job well done and we all know from experience that when the route of the Tour is cleverly conceived, it inspires the competitors.

We are already looking into what the Centennial edition will be, in 2003. One certainty, there will be no revolution in what gives a cycling race its credibility—equal chances offered to all types of riders, which is our responsibility; as well as the sincerity of the competition, which is the responsibility of the competitors, their management and the governing bodies of the sport, with regard to the regulations.

Another certainty, the 2003 Tour de France will be a celebration—in Paris and the Paris region, at the departure and at the finish, but also in the stage towns, and in the symbolic places that we will not miss visiting. A celebration with you and for you, our spectators and television viewing audience. Yes, the Centennial edition will be the occasion for us to show once again there is a connection between the Tour's heart and its public memory.

The 21 teams of the 89th Tour de France

U.S. POSTAL SERVICE
Directeur sportif: BRUYNEEL Johan

1•ARMSTRONG Lance	USA
2•EKIMOV Viatcheslav	Rus
3•HERAS Roberto	Sp
4•HINCAPIE George	USA
5•JOACHIM Benoît	Lux
6•LANDIS Floyd	USA
7•PADRNOS Pavel	Cz
8•PEÑA Victor Hugo	Col
9•RUBIERA José Luis	Sp

KELME-COSTA BLANCA
Directeur sportif: BELDA Vicente

31•SEVILLA Oscar	Sp
32•BOTERO Santiago	Col
33•CABELLO Francisco	Sp
34•GOMEZ CONZALO José Javier	Sp
35•GUTIERREZ José Enrique	Sp
36•PEREZ Santiago	Sp
37•TAULER Antonio	Sp
38•VIDAL José Angel	Sp
39•ZABALLA Constantino	Sp

CRÉDIT AGRICOLE
Directeur sportif: LEGEAY Roger

61•MOREAU Christophe	F
62•BESSY Frédéric	F
63•HINAULT Sébastien	F
64•HUSHOVD Thor	Nor
65•LANGELLA Anthony	F
66•MORIN Anthony	F
67•O'GRADY Stuart	Aus
68•VAUGHTERS Jonathan	USA
69•VOIGT Jens	G

TEAM TELEKOM
Directeur sportif: PEVENAGE Rudy

11•ZABEL Erik	G
12•ALDAG Rolf	G
13•BÖLTS Udo	G
14•FAGNINI Gian Matteo	I
15•GUERINI Giuseppe	I
16•HONDO Danilo	G
17•JULICH Bobby	USA
18•LIVINGSTON Kevin	USA
19•WESEMANN Steffen	G

COFIDIS
Directeur sportif: QUILFEN Bernard

41•KIVILEV Andreï	Kaz
42•ATIENZA Daniel	Sp
43•CUESTA Inigo	Sp
44•FERNANDEZ Bingen	Sp
45•LELLI Massimiliano	I
46•MATTAN Nico	B
47•MILLAR David	GB
48•MONCOUTIÉ David	F
49•VASSEUR Cédric	F

DOMO-FARM FRITES
Directeur sportif: SERGEANT Marc

71•VIRENQUE Richard	F
72•BRUYLANDTS Dave	B
73•CASSANI Enrico	I
74•KNAVEN Servais	Nl
75•KONECNY Tomas	Cz
76•MERCKX Axel	B
77•RODRIGUEZ Fred	USA
78•VAN BON Leon	Nl
79•WADECKI Piotr	Pl

ONCE-EROSKI
Directeur sportif: SAIZ Manolo

21•BELOKI Joseba	Sp
22•AZEVEDO José	P
23•GONZALEZ DE GALDEANO Alvaro	Sp
24•GONZALEZ DE GALDEANO Igor	Sp
25•JAKSCHE Jörg	G
26•NOZAL Isidro	Sp
27•OLANO Abraham	Sp
28•PRADERA Mikel	Sp
29•SERRANO Marcos	Sp

TEAM CSC-TISCALI
Directeur sportif: RIIS Bjarne

51•JALABERT Laurent	F
52•HAMILTON Tyler	USA
53•PERON Andrea	I
54•PIIL Jakob	Dk
55•PIZIKS Arvis	Lat
56•SANDSTÖD Michael	Dk
57•SASTRE Carlos	Sp
58•SÖRENSEN Nicki	Dk
59•VAN HYFTE Paul	B

FASSA BORTOLO
Directeur sportif: FERRETTI Giancarlo

81•BASSO Ivan	I
82•BALDATO Fabio	I
83•BELLI Wladimir	I
84•GUSTOV Volodymir	Ukr
85•HONCHAR Serhiy	Ukr
86•IVANOV Sergueï	Rus
87•LODA Nicola	I
88•POZZI Oscar	I
89•VELO Marco	I

FDJEUX.COM

Directeur sportif: MADIOT Marc

91•VOGONDY Nicolas	F
92•CASAR Sandy	F
93•CASPER Jimmy	F
94•COOKE Baden	Aus
95•DURAND Jacky	F
96•GUESDON Frédéric	F
97•McGEE Bradley	Aus
98•MENGIN Christophe	F
99•ROBIN Jean-Cyril	F

iBANESTO.COM

Directeur sportif: UNZUE Eusebio

131•MENCHOV Denis	Rus
132•BARANOWSKI Dariusz	Pl
133•BLANCO Santiago	Sp
134•BRUSEGHIN Marzio	I
135•GARCIA ACOSTA J. Vincente	Sp
136•LATASA David	Sp
137•MANCEBO Francisco	Sp
138•OSA Unaï	Sp
139•PASCUAL RODRIGUEZ Javier	Sp

TACCONI SPORT

Directeur sportif: ALGERI Vittorio

171•FRIGO Dario	I
172•APOLLONIO Massimo	I
173•BORTOLAMI Gianluca	I
174•BOSSONI Paolo	I
175•DONATI Massimo	I
176•HAUPTMAN Andrej	Slo
177•LUTTENBERGER Peter	A
178•MAZZOLENI Eddy	I
179•RADAELLI Mauro	I

RABOBANK

Directeur sportif: DE ROOY Theo

101•LEIPHEIMER Levi	USA
102•BOOGERD Michaël	Nl
103•DE GROOT Bram	Nl
104•DEKKER Erik	Nl
105•ENGELS Addy	Nl
106•KROON Karsten	Nl
107•NIERMANN Grischa	G
108•WAUTERS Marc	B
109•ZBERG Beat	Swi

LOTTO-ADECCO

Directeur sportif: BRAECKEVELT Jos

141•VERBRUGGHE Rik	B
142•AERTS Mario	B
143•BAGUET Serge	B
144•BRANDT Christophe	B
145•DE CLERCQ Hans	B
146•MARICHAL Thierry	B
147•McEWEN Robbie	Aus
148•MIKHAÏLOV Guennadi	Rus
149•VIERHOUTEN Aart	Nl

AG2R-PRÉVOYANCE

Directeur sportif: LAVENU Vincent

181•BOTCHAROV Alexandre	Rus
182•AGNOLUTTO Christophe	F
183•BERGÈS Stéphane	F
184•CHAURREAU Iñigo	Sp
185•FLICKINGER Andy	F
186•KIRSIPUU Jaan	Est
187•LODER Thierry	F
188•ORIOL Christophe	F
189•TURPIN Ludovic	F

BONJOUR

Directeur sportif: BERNAUDEAU Jean-René

111•ROUS Didier	F
112•BÉNÉTEAU Walter	F
113•BOUYER Franck	F
114•CHAVANEL Sylvain	F
115•MAGNIEN Emmanuel	F
116•NAZON Damien	F
117•PINEAU Jérôme	F
118•RENIER Franck	F
119•SIMON François	F

LAMPRE-DAIKIN

Directeur sportif: ALGERI Pietro

151•SERPELLINI Marco	I
152•BELOHVOSCIKS Raivis	Lat
153•BERTOGLIATI Rubens	Swi
154•CORTINOVIS Alessandro	I
155•DIERCKXSENS Ludo	B
156•PAGLIARINI Luciano	Bra
157•PINOTTI Marco	I
158•RUMSAS Raimondas	Lit
159•SVORADA Jan	Cz

ALESSIO

Directeur sportif: CENGHIALTA Bruno

191•DUFAUX Laurent	Swi
192•BROGNARA Andrea	I
193•CASAGRANDA Stefano	I
194•CASAROTTO Davide	I
195•GOTTI Ivan	I
196•HVASTIJA Martin	Slo
197•IVANOV Ruslan	Mol
198•MORENI Cristian	I
199•SHEFER Alexandr	Kaz

MAPEI-QUICK STEP

Directeur sportif: PARSANI Serge

121•FREIRE Oscar	Sp
122•BODROGI Laszlo	Hun
123•DE WAELE Fabien	B
124•HORRILLO Pedro	Sp
125•HUNTER Robert	SA
126•MARTINEZ Miguel	F
127•STEELS Tom	B
128•TAFI Andrea	I
129•TRAMPUSCH Gerhardt	A

EUSKALTEL-EUSKADI

Directeur sportif: GOROSPE Julian

161•ETXEBARRIA David	Sp
162•ARRIZABALAGA Gorka	Sp
163•ETXEBARRIA Unaï	Ven
164•FLORES Igor	Sp
165•GONZALEZ Gorka	Sp
166•LAISEKA Roberto	Sp
167•MAYO Iban	Sp
168•SANCHEZ Samuel	Sp
169•ZUBELDIA Haimar	Sp

JEAN DELATOUR

Directeur sportif: GROS Michel

201•HALGAND Patrice	F
202•AUGÉ Stéphane	F
203•BERNARD Jérôme	F
204•BROCHARD Laurent	F
205•DESSEL Cyril	F
206•EDALEINE Christophe	F
207•GOUBERT Stéphane	F
208•LEFÈVRE Laurent	F
209•SEIGNEUR Eddy	F

89TH TOUR DE FRANCE
JULY 6TH TO JULY 28TH

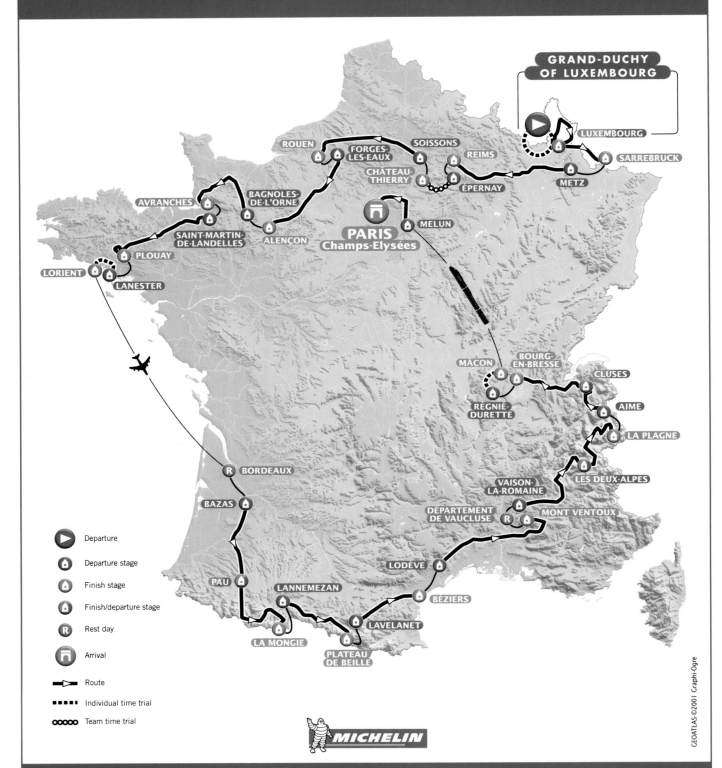

GRAND-DUCHY OF LUXEMBOURG

LUXEMBOURG
SARREBRUCK
ROUEN
FORGES-LES-EAUX
SOISSONS
REIMS
CHÂTEAU-THIERRY
ÉPERNAY
METZ
AVRANCHES
BAGNOLES-DE-L'ORNE
SAINT-MARTIN-DE-LANDELLES
ALENÇON
PARIS Champs-Elysées
MELUN
PLOUAY
LORIENT
LANESTER
MÂCON
BOURG-EN-BRESSE
CLUSES
RÉGNIÉ-DURETTE
AIME
LA PLAGNE
LES DEUX-ALPES
VAISON-LA-ROMAINE
BORDEAUX
DÉPARTEMENT DE VAUCLUSE
MONT VENTOUX
BAZAS
LODÈVE
PAU
LANNEMEZAN
BÉZIERS
LA MONGIE
LAVELANET
PLATEAU DE BEILLE

Departure
Departure stage
Finish stage
Finish/departure stage
Rest day
Arrival
Route
Individual time trial
Team time trial

MICHELIN

GEOATLAS ©2001 Graphi-Ogre

2002 HIGHLIGHTS

THE GRAND-DUCHY EPIC

By launching the race in Luxembourg for a second time in the Tour's history, the organizers honored a nation that has played an important role in the chronicles of cycling. Small in size, but of incomparable economic, cultural, and sporting richness, the peaceful country of Luxembourg has one of the highest concentrations of top cyclists in the world.

Rooted in a century of history, the Tour de France is made up of traditions, like the official inauguration: the Grand Duke of Luxembourg bows to the occasion.

With some 400,000 inhabitants, Luxembourg has produced talented riders since the birth of bike racing in the late 1800s.

The Tour de France record of Luxembourg's cyclists is exemplary—four final victories, sixty-three stage wins, two best climber titles. François Faber, the magnanimous champion, was a marvelous pioneer. This gentle giant, who died on the Artois battlefield in World War I, was the Tour's first non-French winner in 1909. Nicolas Frantz triumphed twice, in 1927 and 1928, when he wore the yellow jersey from beginning to end and gave himself the supreme satisfaction of winning the final stage.

However, the most sensational exploit of a racer from Luxembourg remains that of Charly Gaul, who overcame a seemingly insurmountable lead on the final mountain stage through a rainstorm in the Chartreuse massif in 1958. The race followers of that time have not forgotten how he demolished his final rivals, including the Italian Vito Favero (third on the stage at ten minutes) and the Frenchman Raphaël Geminiani (who lost more than fifteen minutes and the yellow jersey). Gaul, referred to as the "Angel of the Mountains," had already won the 1956 Giro d'Italia in a snowstorm on Monte Bondone. This time, he let loose in an icy rain that pelted the riders for more than six hours and blew the race apart.

Forty-four years after this memorable episode, Lance Armstrong presented Gaul with the polka-dot jersey for the best climber—a jersey that didn't exist in his day. It was a doubly symbolic gesture, as the two champions are both legendary mountain climbers who excel in cold weather conditions.

Besides Faber, Frantz, and Gaul, the honor roll of cyclists from the Grand Duchy includes Arsène Mersch, Jean Majérus, Pierre and Mathias Clémens, Jean Goldschmit, Jempy Schmitz, Willy Kemp, Jean Kirchen, Johny Schleck, Eddy Schutz, and Bim Diederich—who won fame on Fausto Coppi's team. The late Elsy Jacobs was the first woman to win a world championship (in 1958), as well as the first official holder of the women's world hour record. The Paris-Luxembourg stage race, promoted by the radio and television network RTL and former French racer Jean Bobet, was a great cycling event in the 1960s and 1970s.

Luxembourg City is the only foreign capital to take pride in twice hosting the start of the Tour de France, the first time twelve years after the prologue victory of Erik Breukink in the 1989 edition. For Jean-Marie Leblanc, who praised the excellence and friendliness of the Luxembourg reception committee, this Tour rendezvous in the Grand Duchy was also a special pilgrimage for the race's director general, who wore the leader's jersey in the 1969 Tour du Luxembourg.

Luxembourg has recorded 4 final victories, 63 stage wins, and 2 best climber titles.

When two champions meet, respect can be read on their faces: Lance Armstrong presents the best climber jersey to Charly Gaul, of Luxembourg, who won the Tour de France in 1958.

Upon his arrival in Luxembourg, Lance Armstrong seemed more determined than ever. Whether in front of a microphone or on a bicycle, he's a hard hitter.

Engaged in the anti-doping battle, the organizers of the Tour de France defend the ethics of the sport. Simple principles are recited aloud by Jérôme Pineau, the youngest rider of the Tour, at the start of the first stage.

Each time that it goes beyond French borders, the Tour de France attracts crowds and gives rise to mass excitement; Luxembourg was no exception to the rule.

The race has barely begun and already the stars and stripes hang over the Tour.

2 Prologue

ARMSTRONG LAUNCHES THE TOUR

Since his stunning prologue victory in 1999, Armstrong had apparently lost his talent for winning opening time trials.

At the 2000 Tour, he was narrowly defeated on the 16.5-kilometer time trial by David Millar at Futuroscope. In 2001, the 8.2-kilometer prologue victory went to Christophe Moreau in Dunkirk. And at the 2002 Dauphiné Libéré, he failed to win the brief opener. But in Luxembourg, Armstrong put an end to a situation that could have become embarrassing.

After a fierce effort of nine minutes and a few seconds on the technical, figure-eight Luxembourg circuit, the triple winner of the Tour de France won a clear victory and the first yellow jersey of the race. Such an athletic achievement is in keeping with the Armstrong legend, since we could hardly imagine the peloton's best rider being robbed of the victory in such a difficult time trial. Did the American champion—known to be a perfectionist—aim at reassuring himself or was he fighting his eternal skepticism, which has proven to be a strength rather than a weakness?

The triple winner of the Tour de France won a clear victory and the first yellow jersey of the race.

Whatever his goal, Armstrong had an excellent race on a dynamic course that required the racers to repeatedly accelerate out of tight turns and up short climbs. Laurent Jalabert worked wonders in this tough task to finish second, a rank less surprising than that of Lithuanian Raimondas Rumsas, who took third place. Only seven riders, including Millar, Santiago Botero, Dario Frigo, and Igor Gonzalez de Galdeano, conceded less than ten seconds to the winner.

In a good position at the end of the prologue, Igor Gonzalez de Galdeano will soon take the yellow jersey, the first Spaniard since Indurain to do so.

Lance Armstrong at work: power, velocity, precision, concentration. For the man and champion riding at 45 kph, an ideal start to the Tour.

Following the example of the Australian Cadel Evans, a mountain-bike crossover, the Frenchman Miguel Martinez launched himself into an honorable road racing career.

Joseba Beloki didn't have any illusions at the start of this Tour, Lance Armstrong was too strong an opponent. The Spaniard was racing for second place.

Everyone believed it would happen: Jalabert in yellow at the end of the prologue! But Armstrong decided otherwise.

3 Portrait

THE RUBENS TOUCH

Rubens Bertogliati won the media battle and made a name for himself at the 2002 Tour.

At our side, former Tour riders Maurice Le Guilloux and Serge Guyot had the same reaction. And they were quick to mention the names of Jean Forestier, Rudi Altig, Willy Teirlinck, and Jelle Nijdam—rare hard hitters who were capable, in their time, of such final-kilometer attacks.

For the record, prior to this edition of the Tour, only five Swiss riders had won the opening stage: Michel Frederick in 1904, Paul Egli in 1936, Ferdi Kubler in 1947, Giovanni Rossi in 1951, and Fritz Schaer in 1953. Rubens Bertogliati stands out among his elder countrymen. Well-read and educated, he speaks German, Italian, English, and French—an inestimable asset for the countless interviews he will now have to give.

Taking the first stage by surprise, with as much nerve as panache, the twenty-three-year-old Swiss road racer's name was immediately recorded in the annals of cycling.

We knew very little about Bertogliati prior to his amazing feat on Sunday, July 7. A native of Lugano, a beautiful lakeside town near the Italian border, he played soccer before turning to cycling and then graduated from high school between races. His debut Tour de France in 2001 was a discreet, if not confident exercise of preparation. Now, suddenly, his name has appeared at the top of the bill. How did he achieve this exploit, and cause a stir among the most indifferent spectators?

In the last uphill kilometer, he broke away from a pack being paced at a speed that seemed to prohibit such an effort. Bertogliati created a fifty-meter gap and held on for the win by unknowingly following the seventy-year-old principle of the French Pélissier brothers: *Attack as late as possible, but always before the others.* Better still, Bertogliati enjoyed the added luxury of taking the yellow jersey.

"Tremendous!" exclaimed our driver Christian Boulnois, an expert on the subject. "He was brilliant. I wonder where he got the energy to charge away like that."

An angel face and extraordinary talents: Bertogliati was a surprise at the start of this Tour.

Clearly, pink and yellow don't go together very well, but Rubens Bertogliati wouldn't part with his precious leader's jersey.

A snaking peloton in lush Luxembourg.

4 Opinion

VICTIM OF FATE . . . AND AN EAR PIECE

The yellow jersey slipped away in the Luxembourg prologue at the very last minute; it vanished in the final kilometer of the first stage, once again eluding the French racer Laurent Jalabert in the finale of the team time trial. Jalabert's great loss was Spaniard Igor Gonzalez de Galdeano's happy gain. It was a day unlike any other.

The Tour de France combines all forms of road racing and the collective time trial illustrates the spectrum of cycling. The team time trial is a fundamental discipline according to the technicians and a subtle art in the eyes of the purists and real aficionados, who affirm that this exercise in technique is to bicycle racing what ballet is to classical dancing. In a certain way it justifies the expression used in the past by Antonin Magne, Tour winner in 1931 and 1934. He compared the Tour de France to a spider's web: "You have to patiently spin and not miss a stitch." This can also apply to team time trials, as they rarely allow for mistakes. Laurent Jalabert knows this only too well.

A hesitation, a wavering, tactical indecision following Michael Sandstöd's very unfortunate puncture twenty kilometers before the finish deprived Jalabert of a yellow jersey virtually acquired and without a doubt deserved. His CSC-Tiscali team was in control from the start in Épernay, heading for a victory that would have ensured the Frenchman's triumph. When the fatal incident took place, at kilometer forty-six of the sixty-seven-kilometer stage, they were ten seconds ahead of ONCE and twenty seconds in front of Lance Armstrong's U.S. Postal Service squad. Should they wait for Sandstöd? A good question, and an unfortunate answer. Bjarne Riis, the former Tour champion and now CSC's directeur sportif, asked his men to slow down, contrary to what would be expected in this situation. The talented Danish time-trialist was then unable to re-establish contact on the team's course communications radio, his spirit now broken and motivation spent. CSC-Tiscali wouldn't recover from this scarcely comprehensible mistake. The damage was done. It was in vain that the remaining seven men sped up, even if they took back a few seconds—the precision is interesting—during the last five kilometers. They ended up in third place, forty-six seconds behind the ONCE-Eroski pace setters. U.S. Postal, second by sixteen seconds, played their game well. CSC's deplorable failure, or should we say wasted chance, re-launched the debate over earpieces condemned by most former champions, from Jean Bobet to Raymond Poulidor.

In 2000 in Saint-Nazaire, the ONCE team won the team time trial and its leader Laurent Jalabert took the yellow jersey. ONCE won again in 2002, but this time it prevented CSC's Jalabert from taking yellow.

The Danish team CSC-Tiscali was obviously strong, but fate decided otherwise. An unfortunate puncture and the hopes of France were dashed. Jalabert wouldn't wear the yellow jersey for his last Tour de France. Sometimes, talent is not enough.

Telecommunication within the pack is the best and the worst thing. The benefits that may be obtained cannot erase the problems caused. Jalabert, very unlucky in this Tour de France, was the victim of a technique that eclipses

CSC-Tiscali wouldn't recover from this scarcely comprehensible mistake. The damage was done.

personal initiative and can eventually backfire.

Jalabert's misfortune was another's fortune, that of Prince Igor, alias Gonzalez de Galdeano, leader of an ONCE-Eroski team faithful to its reputation. The Spanish riders' harmony and unity allowed them a faultless race, with a remarkable average speed of 50.7 kph on an extremely demanding course.

United, compact, motivated, and disciplined, Lance Armstrong's team came close to winning, but, as in previous years, they fell short in this perilous team time trial.

Did the disagreement between the French champion and his director Bjarne Riis hasten Jalabert's decision to end his career? A gentleman reveals nothing.

A model of cohesion, the Spanish team Once placed four riders in the first five of the overall classification and eight in the top fifteen: who could ask for more?

Erik Zabel, who lost the yellow jersey in Château-Thierry, really only thinks about the green jersey. Green and yellow… like the colors of the Australian champion, his rival Robbie McEwen.

5 Close Up

WHEN THE FRENCH ARE SINGLE-MINDED . . .

From Luxembourg to Brittany, from the country that pedals to the region that cultivates a passion for cycling, the 2002 Tour overturned traditional theories and preconceived ideas. It all began with the festivities in the Grand Duchy, and its bucolic setting—or its "living watercolors," as our colleague from the French newspaper *Le Figaro*, aptly described it.

Upon leaving Luxembourg, we came upon colossal crowds lining the German roads in the hot sun—a remarkable gathering of enthusiastic spectators, never before seen in the Tour. Passing through the Lorraine region we raced as fast as possible toward Reims, the town where France has crowned kings and champions, to the rhythm of a race as sparkling as the best Reims champagne.

Those who envisioned a repeat of the 2001 Tour were somewhat short sighted. Early in the race there was an offensive that brought a new generation of French road racers to the forefront: Sylvain Chavanel, Stéphane Bergès, Franck Renier, Sandy Casar, Anthony Morin, Stéphane Augé, Laurent Lefèvre, and Christophe Edalaine. Their appetite for obstinate resistance to being caught would have them classified by the late, distinguished French author Antoine Blondin as "single-minded."

Unfortunately, perseverance isn't always justly rewarded. Franck Renier, who broke away from the pack along with the inevitable Jacky Durand in the Normandy countryside, couldn't manage a breakthrough in Avranches. He was caught only two kilometers from the finish (the stage won by McGee), but he had the satisfaction of being the virtual yellow jersey during this long breakaway, and in the end he took leadership of the most aggressive rider classification.

The roads of Brittany are known to invite such long breaks. One of the more memorable offensives involved four riders considered to be favorites in the 1960 Tour. Gastone Nencini, Roger Rivière, Hans Junkermann, and Jan Adriaenssens left the main pack of cyclists fifteen minutes behind. The Breton rider Sébastien Hinault wanted to use this same terrain in the 2002 Tour to dominate the stage. A Bastille Day finish in Plouay was an opportunity not to be missed, particu-

Sylvain Chavanel and Stéphane Bergès received an incredible German welcome on the way to Saarbrucken.

Frenchmen were in nearly all the breakaways, like Anthony Morin or Sébastien Hinault, who revived legend on the roads of Brittany, a land where the men have character.

larly for a rider from the region. However, Hinault's most sincere intentions were not realized, leaving him to face his disappointment.

Hinault was in the conclusive attack, launched long before the finish was within reach, and involving three Frenchmen (Hinault, Rénier, and Augé) and three Dutchmen (Karsten Kroon, Erik Dekker, and Servais Knaven). In the end, the visitors proved the champions, and they swept the first three places. The impressive victory by Kroon, one of the big hopes of the Dutch cycling, literally wiped out the homeboys. In their desire to affirm themselves, their efforts were great; too great, perhaps. This breath-

taking eighth stage was exhausting, both physically and mentally—ninety-eight kilometers were covered during the first two hours and the average speed was

Those who envisioned a repeat of the 2001 Tour were somewhat short sighted.

47.135 kph. And it is probably this continual tension that condemned the three Frenchmen, who proved less resistant, less hardened, and less inspired than Kroon, Dekker, and Knaven.

It was in Pau, on the eleventh day of racing, that the French recorded a first success with Patrice Halgand taking the stage. In this opening phase of the Tour there were many crashes, which eliminated Tom Steels, Didier Rous, and world champion Oscar Freire. There was also the incident—almost derisory within the overall context of the Tour—which could have had heavier consequences: a collision at the entrance to Avranches that cost Lance Armstrong (and Jalabert) twenty-seven seconds.

With the Tour's first act drawing to a close, the Pyrénées loomed on the horizon, and the pack was already close to breaking up.

"What a devil!" Christophe Edaleine seems to be saying to himself, at the head of the breakaway moving victoriously toward Rouen. Sometimes, the public puts on a show for the riders.

LE TOUR DE FRANCE

Two leaders in danger: Igor Gonzalez de Galdeano and Erik Zabel know that Armstrong and McEwen are hot on their heels. As is always the case, adversity gives rise to complicity.

The Tour heroes are cheered on by the kids, who appreciate the PMU green hand.

When the pack crosses the pastoral countryside of Normandy, the Tour de France looks like a quiet bicycle trip; but between Saint-Martin-de-Landelles and Plouay the pace will be intense and the stage covered at an average 47.135 kph!

"Luck is like the Tour de France: we wait for it for a long time, but it passes quickly." *(Amélie)*

Between heaven and earth, between blue and green, Casagranda, Sandstod, Dierckxsens, Edaleine and Kirsipuu have shaken off the pack and will reap the rewards of their efforts a little later on: an even battle and a stage victory for the Estonian sprinter.

A rare picture on the 2002 Tour: the peloton riding slowly, like a comet with a long multicolored tail crossing the most beautiful regions of France.

6 Retrospective

1952: COPPI, THE ALPE D'HUEZ, AND TELEVISION.

It was fifty years ago. Dwight Eisenhower, the World War II hero, was settling in at the White House, while the mysterious Dominic affair shook Antoine Pine's peaceful France. Hemingway published *The Old Man and The Sea* and people lined up outside cinemas to see *Singing in the Rain* and *Basque Door.*

Also an exceptional year for the Tour de France, 1952 was full of innovative and heroic exploits—the best Tour of modern times, according to the late cycling historian Pierre Chany. The innovation came with the first summit finishes, destined to highlight climbers' performances, and truly one of the greatest additions of the last half-century. Three mountaintop finishes thus made their debut, alongside the old classics typified by the Tourmalet or the Galibier: the Alpe d'Huez, Sestriere, and the Puy-de-Dôme. It was also in 1952, when French television first became part of the Tour caravan, at the initiative of Pierre Sabaggh and Georges De Caunes.

In the 1952 race, Fausto Coppi flew over the competition, winning first on Alpe d'Huez, then at Sestriere, and finally at the top of the Puy-de-Dôme. It was a dominating performance unique to the history of the Tour. By the finish in Paris, the Italian *campionissimo* was ahead of his nearest rival, Belgian Stan Ockers, by 28:17—the

In 1952, the organizers first introduced mountain top finishes; the *campionissimo* simplifies the task of cycling historians by winning the three mountain stages, always in the same way, by taking off in the final ascent.

The Tour de France was broadcast on television for the first time in 1952. Over the space of fifty years and via the magic of satellite, it has become a global event.

In the 1952 race, Fausto Coppi flew over the competition, winning first on Alpe d'Huez, then at Sestriere, and finally at the top of the Puy-de-Dôme.

greatest gap in the last half-century. Rik Van Steenbergen won the first stage and Nello Lauredi was at the top of the general classification before Coppi arrived on the scene. One of his teammates, the faithful but modest Andrea Carrea, took the yellow jersey by mistake and with the Alps looming on the horizon, he excused himself to shed tears over a trophy that he deemed himself unworthy to have. Coppi comforted him at once and blamed the Italian journalists, who had accused the "poor *gregario* of an unforgivable crime of *lèse-majesté*." "How dare you reproach him this moment of happiness," Coppi exclaimed, at the height of indignation. "He deserved it more than anyone and I'm happy that he has experienced, once in his life, the honors of the podium. His happiness is mine."

37

Contrary to appearances, Sylvain Chavanel, Thor Hushovd, and Stéphane Bergès were more than shadows of their former selves: their cavalcade through the Sarre region almost took the pack by surprise.

Between Metz and Reims, no one has found the secret weapon to slip away from the pack. The teams of sprinters are keeping their eyes open.

A contest of style within the pack, where the rainbow colors worn by Oscar Freire and Laurent Jalabert remind us that the Tour de France reunites the best riders from around the world.

BOTERO'S DAY OF GLORY

Following in the footsteps of two well known yet unheralded South Americans—Lucho Herrera, winner of the Alpe d'Huez stage in 1984, and Fabio Parra, third overall in 1988—Santiago Botero achieved a third exploit for South America by beating Lance Armstrong in the Lorient time trial, becoming the first Colombian to win a Tour de France time-trial stage.

It was a spectacular result, but one that didn't come as a great surprise since the Kelme team rider had already defeated Armstrong in a similar time trial at the Dauphiné Libéré race.

At the Tour de France however, Botero's finish caused a sensation. To achieve the best time, Botero rode at 50.080 kph, a speed that ranks among the greatest individual performances in a time trial. Only eleven seconds separated the first two riders at the finish, but over a distance of fifty-two kilometers, Botero was ahead of Beloki by 1:38, Laurent Jalabert by 3:33, Richard Virenque by 4:23, and Christophe Moreau by 4:40. The first Frenchman, Antony Morin, came in thirtieth, almost three minutes later. Fifty or so riders lost more than seven minutes. From one extreme to the other, last place went to the Dutchman Kroon, who was the previous day's stage winner in Plouay.

Santiago Botero passes by them so quickly that the public appears to clap late and look the wrong way: the Colombian, triumphant on the first individual time-trial, has just overtaken the competitor who set off two minutes before him.

The Brittany time-trial stage emphasised the growing value of the Ukrainian Sergei Gontchar and the Lithuanian Raimondas Rumsas. Renowned for his qualities as a time trialist, Gontchar was in the lead at the twentieth kilometer, and hung onto the third place at the end, only seventeen

> **To achieve the best time, Botero rode at 50.080 kph, a speed that ranks among the greatest individual performances in a time trial.**

seconds back. As for Rumsas, the revelation of the prologue and the Tour, he lost only twenty-five seconds to Botero. However, the star was clearly Botero, who is far from being a typical Colombian cyclist. He is the most European of the Andean riders. With his morphology, his power and his style, he has more in common with Miguel Induráin than with Herrera. Botero has the build and the authority of a company director, and it is fitting that once his career in cycling is over, he aspires to be a director himself. In the meantime, he brightened the pack and provided the Tour followers with new excitement. The late race director Jacques Goddet would have liked the way that this athlete epitomizes the globalization of cycling—an ideal that Goddet strongly supported.

Igor Gonzalez de Galdeano concedes only eight seconds to his rival Lance Armstrong in the time trial. After the stage, the yellow jersey still eludes the American.

Wearing the best climber jersey weighs heavy on the shoulders of Christophe Mengin, who tenuously launches himself from the start ramp.

The fans in Brittany chose traditional hats, while Lance Armstrong went with the customary aero helmet in the time trial.

Second in Paris, the Spaniard Joseba Beloki hopes to some-day win the Tour in 2003 or later?

The Tour de France likes to cross Brittany, a land of cycling. By stopping in Plouay and in Lorient, the Tour made the Brittany public very happy.

Finishing thirty-ninth at 3:29, Isidro Nozal lost his battle with David Millar, to whom he conceded the best young rider's white jersey.

The time trial is a long battle against pain, a test of personal limits that certain riders fear more than anything. The South African Robert Hunter, whose multicolored jersey matches the local colors, doesn't seem ready to take the start.

The roads of the 2002 Tour were invaded by enthusiastic and friendly crowds, a popular success that greatly rewards the Tour de France organizers.

Undeniably, the Euskatel-Euskadi team failed their Tour, incapable of repeating the exploit of their leader Laiseka, who in 2001 won the Luz-Ardiden stage.

8 Endurance

ARMSTRONG AND JALABERT, HEROES OF THE PYRÉNÉES

Hitting hard from the start has become the trademark of Lance Armstrong.

In 2001, the American attacked on the first appearance of the mountain passes to win back-to-back alpine stages (Alpe d'Huez and Chamrousse), confirming his superiority in the space of twenty-four hours. This scenario, now a classic, was repeated in 2002 when the Pyrénées followed eleven days of racing on the flat. Armstrong didn't hang around, but he didn't give way to impatience. He was coldly determined, knowing exactly what he needed to do. True to his method, he made his move when he was ready. Everything went as planned, with a timed precision that nothing and no one could have deterred.

As foreseen, he arrived alone at La Mongie, on the slopes of the Tourmalet, where Bernard Thévenet won his first mountain stage thirty-two years prior. Paced by an amazing Roberto Heras, who accomplished an enormous job throughout the climb, Armstrong emerged just before the finish banner to take the yellow jersey from Gonzalez de Galdeano (who lost 1:54 over the last five kilometers). For the third time in four years, after his attacks on Sestriere in 1999 and Alpe d'Huez in 2001, Armstrong thus won the first mountain stage. It was a way of affirming that he was the boss, just in case we'd forgotten.

Once more, this exploit called for a repeat—an opportunity for Armstrong to win a new psychological battle and gain extra points over the opposition. Without hesitation he triumphed the following day, high on the Plateau-de-Beille, just as he had triumphed at La Mongie. The pattern of this second stage in the Pyrénées was just like the first. In pursuit of Jalabert, who had made a long breakaway for the second time in two days, he caught up with the Frenchman nine kilometers from the finish and went on alone, with a little over six kilometers to cover. By the finish, the U.S. Postal leader was 1:04 ahead of Heras and Spain's Joseba Beloki, who was now his primary challenger. At the exit to the Pyrénées, Armstrong was leading by 2:28.

We can't discuss the Pyrénées without linking Laurent Jalabert to Lance Armstrong, because the two men were the true heroes of these two stages. With a sharp eye for opportunities, Jalabert also managed to repeat his magnificent performance of 2001. Aware that he

Armstrong and Jalabert were the two heroes of this 2002 Tour. One of them takes cycling towards new heights, the other takes his leave at the end of the year.

In the first of the two stages in the Pyrénées, Roberto Heras worked phenomenally hard for his leader, a sacrifice that gave Armstrong a stage victory and the yellow jersey.

couldn't play a role in the overall classification, and acting from experience, he once again aimed for the best climber title. With this goal in mind, the popular Jaja didn't select the easiest of challenges. This talented fighter, guided by his race intelligence, was the man of the situation—the only one, perhaps, who could take on this sort of challenge.

We can't discuss the Pyrénées without linking Laurent Jalabert to Lance Armstrong, because the two men were the true heroes of these two stages.

Between Pau and La Mongie, Jalabert launched himself in a 120-kilometer-long raid and he came only 3,500 meters short of winning. However, Jalabert achieved a prestigious coup by leading the race alone at the top of the mighty Aubisque—a great moment in the career of this rider, as highlighted by Philippe Bouvet in the French sports newspaper *L'Équipe*.

Jalabert launched a new offensive the next day, in the company of Christophe Oriol and Laurent Dufaux, which allowed him to cross in first position the Portet d'Aspet, the Col de la Corre pass, and the Col de Port, accumulating more climbing points and earning, as in 2001, the polka-dot jersey. It was only to be expected that he would continue the following day, as the Cathare country passes (his region—particularly the Montségur and St.-Benoît climbs) that are situated at the beginning of the route, allowed him to increase his lead in the best climber standings. Jalabert profited shrewdly from the occasion and came through this three-day adventure with increased stature, wildly applauded by a public willing him on, throughout 430 kilometers of breakaways.

A Frenchman riding under Danish colors and encouraged by Basque supporters: modern cycling offers an international image in line with the world wide media coverage of the Tour de France.

While his two rivals suffer, Lance Armstrong calmly converses with his directeur sportif. Decidedly untouchable.

Heroically, Laurent Jalabert battled to wear a new polka dot jersey and for the status of national hero. Between Pau and La Mongie, he accumulates 46 points in the best climber classification.

An honor guard accompanies the pack on the way from Lannemezan to the Plateau-de-Beille; passion for the Tour, a real religion.

On the slopes of La Mongie, Heras, Armstrong, and Beloki make their way through the Spanish public who encourage the American as though he was one of their own.

Armstrong in the yellow jersey controls the race like a real boss; unlucky in this Tour, Christophe Moreau rarely found himself riding this close to the champion.

Fabio Casartelli must haunt the thoughts of his former teammate, Lance Armstrong, as the pack passes in front of the sculpture that commemorates his fatal accident in 1995.

The "panda" played a new trick on the mountain specialists. Two breakaways in two days in the Pyrénées and the best climber jersey was his!

9 Reverence

PATRICE HALGAND, SHY BUT DARING

It's possible to be shy in other aspects of life yet daring on a bike. Patrice Halgand, who claims to be reserved, has the image of a relaxed rider with no hang ups. In Pau, he won the first French stage victory of the 2002 Tour.

It was an important victory because Pau is a sacred place in the history of cycling. From Binda to Zabel, by way of Vietto, Coppi, Rivière, Kelly, Gimondi, or Hinault, the greatest cycling legends have triumphed in the Béarnaise capital. Halgand's victory was also important because he asserted himself with the authority of a superior. The last French win in Pau was in 1985, achieved by Régis Simon, brother to Pascal and François.

Seventeen years later, Halgand finally put an end to a long series of French defeats with an ardor and a spirit of determination that increased the value of his performance. The hard hitter of the Jean Delatour team had already performed amazing feats at the Four Days of Dunkirk and the Dauphiné Libéré stage races. He also finished third in the French championships in Briançon. Halgand was considered one of the most energetic fighters of the new generation, but on the twelfth day of the 2002 Tour de France, he won the showpiece of his career. He managed to break away in the final kilometers from a vanguard group controlled by Stuart O'Grady, Ludo Dierckxsens, and French champion Nicolas Vogondy. Halgand forced his way through, reminiscent of Erik Dekker, and held off the young Frenchman, Jérôme Pineau, to second place.

The stage across the Landes region, generally considered as a transitional one before the Pyrénées, has often given rise to a procession. This time, in spite of the heat, we were provided with the spectacle of a speed test. More than fifty-four kilometers were ridden during the first hour, and at an average of 48.932 kph, it was the third fastest stage in the history of the Tour.[1]

Unfortunately it wasn't a time for joy. Wednesday, July 17, became a day for mourning when a tragic accident took the life of a seven-year-old boy, who was hit by a vehicle from the publicity caravan, in the middle of the celebration.

1. The records are held by Mario Cipollini with an average 50.355 kph (Laval-Blois in 1999) and Johan Bruyneel, the current directeur sportif of the U.S. Postal Service team, an average of 49.417 kph (Evreux-Amiens in 1993).

Classified forty-ninth in the prologue, 26 seconds from Armstrong, Patrice Halgand arrived to this Tour in good shape and with a desire to prove that the place offered to his team on the Tour wasn't in vain.

Halgand is more a hard hitter than a climber. His natural velocity does wonders on the long slopes, where he wins the polka-dot jersey, a trophy to be taken from him by Jalabert in the Pyrénées.

Patrice Halgand leads the breakaway ahead of Zaballa, the first act in a stage where the French champion sees life through rose tinted glasses.

Act II: Just 7.5 kilometres from the finish, profitting from a slight incline, the day's best climber leaves his opponents glued to the spot.

Act III: At a wild average of 48.932 kph, the leader of the Jean Delatour team achieves the first French victory in the 2002 Tour.

WHERE VIRENQUE AND GAUL MET

Their popularity has made them rivals, even if they maintain a façade of friendship. The continued achievements of Laurent Jalabert, and the public's adoring passion for this sweet champion, have dampened the crowd's enthusiasm for Richard Virenque. The French climber, whose pride is legendary, couldn't face such a situation without reacting.

Following an arduous first week, a knee injury, and a bad patch in the Pyrénées, he reinforced his desire for revenge insisting, "I can be dangerous anytime!"
Was the Ventoux a scheduled objective? Probably. Between the hills of the Lodèvois region and the white summit of the Ventoux, the French rider was in his element. He was competing on terrain he always appreciates, on roads perfumed with lavender and thyme, particularly designed for cycling races, as the organizers of the Grand Prix Midi Libre are aware. The crossing of the Cévennes foothills is always risky, especially when the sun is beating down on the pack. During the 1951 Tour, these tricky climbs witnessed the historical burn-out of the great Fausto Coppi, and they have always rewarded aggressive riders. In the end this promising stage through the Languedoc lived up to expectations. It was a perfect setting for Virenque-the-attacker.

Having often conducted long solo breakaways in the mountains over the past ten years, the former polka-dot jersey winner attacked early before triumphing at the top of the Ventoux. His 202-kilometer breakaway under the sun obviously was not the easiest way to capture this coveted stage, but it was the most realistic one, as it gave him and ten escapees valuable freedom. Baranowski, Botcharov, Edaleine, Hushovd, Morin, Velo, Pradera, Moreni, Augé, Serpellini, and Virenque found themselves twelve minutes ahead of the pack with fifty kilometers to go, when the U.S. Postal blue train gathered speed.

But Virenque had cleverly calculated his shot. As a climber, he could easily get rid of the other ten leaders on the Ventoux.

Did he have something in mind? At the start of the Mount Ventoux stage, Richard Virenque stopped by the Village to put the finishing touches on his haircut.

The Russian rider Alexander Botcharov, second in the stage, was the last to follow him, but he was outdistanced eleven kilometers before the summit. Then began a match between Virenque and Armstrong, who was riding five minutes behind the leader when he reached the renowned Chalet Reynard, located six kilometers from the top. The Frenchman fought hard, suffered greatly, and won a stage that makes him part of the cycling legend. Virenque now shares the happiness and glory of a Ventoux victory with Raymond

The crossing of the Cévennes foothills is always risky, especially when the sun is beating down on the pack.

Poulidor, Eddy Merckx, Bernard Thévenet, and Jean-François Bernard. Cheered on by his numerous fans and boosted by his pride, he accomplished an amazing feat. While climbing, did he see the bearded old man, seated near the summit on a rock, alone and silent among a passionate crowd? It was Charly Gaul, the Luxembourg climber, nicknamed the Angel of the Mountains, who won the Ventoux stage as well as the Tour de France forty-four years prior. The success of Richard the Lionhearted cannot eclipse Armstrong's performance. The yellow jersey, third in the stage, was the fastest Tour rider ever on the Ventoux, more than five minutes faster than Virenque over the twenty-one kilometers between Bédoin and the finishing line. His only mistake was to attack too late. But was it a mistake? Armstrong gained time on his Spanish and Lithuanian rivals and declared that, one day, he will indeed conquer the Ventoux. Should we talk about the rude spectators who insulted the American during the ascent? If so, it is only to condemn their appalling behavior; the American champion deserves respect.

After a 202-kilometer breakaway and a painful climb, France's favorite cyclist dominates at the pinnacle of the most mythical of the Tour summits. The Bald Mount accomodates no weakness, but knows how to reward the brave.

Via bus, caravan, and helicopter, the public gathered at the foot of the Observatory to await the arrival of the Tour de France.

With the sun beating down on Provence, a possible weakening of Armstrong was predicted. The American pushed harder, achieving a magnificient ascension.

Carried by the public, Richard Virenque resists the domination of the yellow jersey and achieves his greatest Tour de France victory. Effort, like the joy to come, reaches its highest level.

11 Summits

THE DUTCH ALPS

Dutch road racers love the Alps. A long-standing affection links them first to the Alpe d'Huez, and when the Tour avoids that famed peak, they find other chances to shine.

This year, the designated objective was La Plagne and the winner was Michaël Boogerd. To be more precise, it was the super-alpine stage, via the Galibier and Madeleine passes. This was the one to win, so we can fully understand the joy and emotion of the Dutch rider as he fell into his wife's arms after crossing the finish line.

Boogerd is a great winner. His victories are never banal. They always have an epic air about them. In 1996, he triumphed at Aix-les-Bains in a violent rainstorm and,

this time, he arrived alone at the summit of La Plagne, at the end of an eighty-five-kilometer solo through the mountains. The flatland racer triumphed on the Tour's highest peaks.

A brief recap of the sequence of events on this extraordinary day: Bruseghin, Botero, Osa, Jalabert, and Boogerd break away on the south side of the Galibier after a cold start (a manner of speaking, as the sun was already burning high in the sky). Botero takes the lead in front of the Henri Desgrange monument, the highest eleva-

tion of the Tour at 2,645 meters. And so ends the first act. In the second act, Boogerd goes ahead alone after leaving Valloire. On the descent of the Télégraphe, he is joined first by O'Grady, then by Hunter and Fagnini. At the heart of the Maurienne valley, a strategic section feared by the riders, the gap widens. The pack is seven minutes away. Act three begins with the first bends of the Madeleine pass: Boogerd, decidedly in top form, attacks again but this time he is alone. At the top, he is three minutes ahead of Jalabert, Miguel Martinez, Iban Mayo, and Ludovic Turpin, 3:55 ahead of O'Grady, 4:45 ahead of Marcos Serrano, and 4:55 ahead of Axel Merckx. The yellow jersey pack is 7:45 behind. The Dutchman, who has discovered a climbing vocation, will keep a little more than one minute's lead, in spite of the late pursuit by Lance Armstrong. "It's the greatest victory of my career," he exclaims with heartfelt exuberance. Yet we haven't forgotten that he is the same racer who has won Paris-Nice and the Amstel Gold Race.

It is obviously impossible to recount this great alpine stage without talking about Jalabert. Third on the Galibier and second on the Madeleine—an almost unhoped-for result—Bjarne Riis's protégé swiped an additional sixty-five mountain points to secure the best climber title. Above all, Laurent-the-Magnificent not only won his polka-dot jersey in category III or IV passes, but his presence at the front on two of the most difficult passes in France was enough to prove that he is worthy of such a title.

To the prize list must be added Martinez the neophyte who battled valiantly, Carlos Sastre who finished well (just ahead of Armstrong), and David Moncoutié who distanced in a decisive way from Virenque, obviously suffering from his ride on the Ventoux.

On the day before, at les Deux-Alpes, we were treated to a spectacle from Botero, the robust Colombian, who was proving to be the most complete and probably the

Tired but not undaunted, Dutchman Michael Boogerd fixes his eyes on the summit, intent on the goal within his reach.

most efficient man in the pack, apart from Armstrong, of course. At an elevation of 1,650 meters Botero was a solo winner—after winning a flat time-trial stage, the former best climber prize-winner has found his favorite terrain. We are not sure if he should be defined as a climber who likes flat races or a flatland racer who climbs. Already a stage winner in Briançon in 2000, the South American strove toward the Deux-Alpes summit after a 170-kilometer breakaway, and then managed to free himself from the two outstanding Belgians who were accompanying him, Axel Merckx and Mario Aerts.

As Bogotá was waking up, Hector Urrego, the RNC radio reporter announced the great news on the airwaves. The leader of the Kelme team had just equaled Lucho Herrera's record by winning his third stage of the Tour de France. "The work of an expert," according to Urrego, "at the height of exaltation—a pure masterpiece." The Boteros from Colombia are decidedly masters of their craft.

Dario Frigo came back to save the day for Italy by winning in Cluses, ahead of Aerts and Guerini, a former Alpe d'Huez hero. As for Moncoutié, now in fourth place well ahead of Virenque, he confirmed his position as the Tour's top Frenchman. And the amazing Laurent Lefèvre was also near the

At the heart of the Maurienne valley, a strategic section feared by the riders, the gap widens.

head of the list. Lance Armstrong crossed the Alps without crossing a finish line in first place. It didn't stop him from keeping his challengers at a distance and knocking them out on occasion, even if his daily counterattacks were too late to succeed. Practically assured of winning his fourth Tour de France upon leaving the Pyrénées, Armstrong adapted his tactics to the circumstances. The long breakaways that developed between the Provence and Savoy regions scarcely threatened him, and no one would dream of reproaching him for his cautious, indeed wary, attitude.

The final mountains claimed some distinguished victims: Dufaux; Guesdon; Casper; Christophe Moreau, the record holder for crashes who gave up on the Deux-Alpes route; and above all Oscar Sevilla, the best young rider in the 2001 Tour and the great hope of Spanish cycling.

The day after his victory, Boogerd can be proud of himself, as all the newspapers praise his incredible epic.

Three successive stages in the Alps tested the riders and provided us with three great winners, the only possible regret being that the race leader was never attacked in the mountains.

Italian Dario Frigo, here at the head of the breakaway, prevents Italy from going home empty handed; but Belgian Mario Aerts put up a great fight.

Colombian Santiago Botero was successfull on all types of terrain, winning a time trial and a mountain stage. Looking to 2003, he could be a formidable rival for Lance Armstrong.

12 A French Hero

MERCI, MONSIEUR JALABERT

"An example and a legend." . . . Lance Armstrong's description of Laurent Jalabert, is undoubtedly befitting a French champion who has written his name in the history of cycling, while at the same time announcing his decision to leave the sport.

It is a sublime epilogue to a career that has proven incomparable in many ways. It has often been said that there was a little of Louison (Bobet) in Jaja, the two men sharing in common a rich record of achievements, a taste for work accomplished, and the panache of Henri Pélissier, the great French rider of the 1920s. Today, we are tempted to compare Jalabert and Bernard Hinault, as they both knew to leave the scene at the height of their success, with the authority of great captains, and the wisdom of stars who refuse to offer their fans the image of an irreversible deterioration. This is a token of elegance and a sign of respect for their public.

Tuesday, July 16, Laurent Jalabert takes advantage of the rest day in Bordeaux to announce his impending retirement. In front of the television cameras, he expresses himself soberly, with phrases filled with dignity and emotion. No nostalgia . . . or very little. Words are spoken from the heart, at times an allusion, a lighthearted joke, a smile through which we see no sadness. The audience is charmed. Jaja thanks the journalists who have devoted so many articles to him; the writers applaud. They rediscover the mutual appreciation that in former times united everyone on the Tour de France voyage, from the riders to the caravan of Tour followers. Hence we learn that Jalabert is participating in his last Tour de France and we know that he will leave with his head held high. He's retiring after mature reflection, he's not resigning and, as Jacques Goddet declared, retirement doesn't quell the passion.

Two days later, Jalabert attacks in the Pyrénées in order to win the polka-dot jersey for the second time running. Far from finished, he repeats last year's daring shot, in exactly the same way, with the same brilliance. Frankly, he amazes us. On the slopes of the Aubisque, he is carried by the crowd. It's sheer madness. At the Plateau-de-Beille, his young opponents form an honor guard and clap when he crosses the finish line. He steals the limelight from Virenque, and, in a certain way, from Lance Armstrong. Placards reappear on the roadsides. We no longer count the number of "Long live Jaja" signs, but new expressions of admiration. He is now called Monsieur: "*Merci, Monsieur Jalabert.*" His fans plead with him: "Don't leave us!" Esteem becomes affection in the messages delivered to him: "Jaja, we love you."

Popular fervor is not only drawn from sentiment, as in the 2002 Tour, which pro-

In Bordeaux, Laurent Jalabert announces he will retire from cycling at the end of the year, an unexpected turn of events.

longs and confirms the 2001 edition, has restored to us the quicksilver rider whose varied list of achievements astonishes the experts. The French road racer, a late bloomer, hasn't stopped widening his range of activities. He has won races as varied as the French National Championship, Milan–San Remo, World Cup events, the Flèche Wallonne, the Classique des Alps, and many stage races such as Paris-Nice, the Midi Libre, and the Vuelta, not to mention the World Time Trial Championship.

Esteem becomes affection in the messages delivered to him: "Jaja, we love you."

Eddy Merckx similarly won the yellow jersey, the green jersey, and the best climber jersey all in the same year, 1969. Bernard Hinault also cast a wide net to have his name included in the record book for points classification and best climber. But do you know of a rider who has won the green jersey and the polka-dot jersey in a ten-year interval, a sprinter who became a climber and who received two Oscars in each discipline? Apart from Jalabert, no one has achieved such feats. Forgotten are the bad moments of his career, the drama of his frightening crash at Armentières, the calamitous end-of-century years. The Tour de France has made this musketeer a happy man, another Poulidor.

Laurent Brochard, David Moncoutié, Richard Virenque, Miguel Martinez, and all the other French riders applaud Laurent as he wraps up an interview with Tour broadcasters—a great tribute!

Richard Virenque wanted to win a new best climber title, but in the Alps and the Pyrénées, he was no more than a shadow of himself and of Jaja, who stole the limelight and the polka-dot jersey from him.

This photograph explains quite a few things: from now on Laurent Jalabert wants to be close to his wife and to see his children grow up.

The best climber and the most aggressive rider in the 2002 Tour, Jaja also received the Photographers' Orange Prize for the nicest rider in the peloton: does he have any faults?

SUPREME HONORS

Supreme honors go to Lance Armstrong. Supreme honors go to Robbie McEwen. In the Beaujolais region, the American put the finishing touches on his triumph by gliding through the last time trial. On the Champs-Elysées, the Australian beat the pack in the sprint and won a symbolic victory that gave his green jersey maximum glory.

Beaten by Botero in Lorient, Armstrong gained revenge in a dazzling way before arriving in the capital. The result of the Régnié-Durette to Mâcon time trial through the Beaujolais vineyards was without appeal. At the height of his glory, the yellow jersey holder beat second-place Rumsas by fifty-three seconds, while Botero, his chief rival, was at 2:11. Millar, the specialist, stopped things from getting any worse by coming in fourth at 1:14. An interesting and very significant detail: David Moncoutié, the top Frenchman in the Tour, was also France's best in this ultimate race of truth. He nevertheless had to settle for twenty-first place, 3:56 behind Armstrong, who covered the fifty kilometers, in unbearable heat, at an average 46.997 kph. Laurent Jalabert was thirtieth at 4:26. Motivations must be taken into account; Jalabert had nothing more to prove as his Tour was finished. Connoisseurs of statistics will note that Armstrong won his fifteenth Tour de France stage—a figure that puts him on the same level as Freddy Maertens, and one win away from Charles Pélissier and Jacques Anquetil.

The other hero of the final weekend was Robbie McEwen. He put an end to Zabel's series of six consecutive wins in the points classification and nearly claimed a

> **Connoisseurs of statistics will note that Armstrong won his fifteenth Tour de France stage—a figure that puts him on the same level as Freddy Maertens, and one win away from Charles Pélissier and Jacques Anquetil.**

historic first victory for Australia in the race for the green jersey. He managed to succeed where his compatriot O'Grady failed in 2001. McEwen left the German, who still threatened him in theory, without the slightest chance; his most serious rival in the final sprint was another Australian, Baden Cooke.

Only seventh in the last stage behind Nazon, Baldato, Casarotto, and O'Grady, Zabel merits the fair-play consolation prize: "No regrets," he declared, "Robbie was faster."

No doubt. On Sunday July 28, McEwen achieved possibly the greatest exploit of his career and the Tour made him the number one road racer-sprinter.

Incredibly focused, Lance Armstrong wins the Mâcon time trial: his power and velocity worked wonders on the vineyard routes.

Finishing third in Paris at 21:08 from the winner, David Moncoutié is the best Frenchman of the 2002 Tour, efficient and discrete, as usual.

Régnié-Durette, Villié-Morgon, Chiroubles, Saint-Amour, Mâcon: here is a route mapped for the connoisseurs of good wine.

The peloton arrives in Paris for the final stretch of the Tour de France.

As in the previous year, the 2002 Tour's green jersey was a tight competition played out in the last stage between German Erik Zabel and an Australian. A coalition seems to plot against the Australian sprinter, but Robbie McEwen wins the stage victory on the Champs-Elysées and is first in the points classification.

Approaching the sprint, McEwen flies by the Place de la Concorde, destined for new success. The Tour has given him wings.

In spite of the fact that the itinerary of the last stage included the Place de la Bastille, there was no revolution to overturn the outcome of the 2002 Tour.

George Hincapie, here with his team leader, sacrificed himself magnificently for three weeks: American cycling is at its peak!

LANCE ARMSTRONG: "I LOVE THE TOUR DE FRANCE!"

On July 26, Lance Armstrong met with a select group of journalists, who were eager to record his impressions two days away from his fourth victory. The following day, in the pressroom, he participated in a session of questions and answers with all of the accredited reporters. Here are some of the things he said:

Question: Over the last four years, have you noticed more Americans lining the roadsides?

Lance Armstrong: Progressively, each year, I do have the impression of seeing more American fans lining the roadsides. They are also more numerous at the finish in Paris, a place that's always been a destination for Americans. On the Champs-Elysées, there are also quite a few people from Austin, and more and more Texas flags.

Q: Many commentators insist that this is the easiest Tour you have won. Do you agree with that analysis?

LA: Frankly, when you have a solid, united team devoted to its leader, it makes life easier. . . . I believe ours is the best team in the peloton and that has helped me a lot over the last three weeks. In reality, their job is much more difficult than mine and as they've done it brilliantly, then yes, this Tour has been the easiest of the four that I have won.

Q: What role has Johan Bruyneel played in your success?

LA: An essential role. I owe him so much, and for so long: first of all, for having believed in me and guessed that I was

The strength and the focus of a great champion: Lance Armstrong already has his eyes set on 2003.

For Armstrong and Bruyneel, complicity stems from a common passion for victory and the celebratory toast that follows.

capable of winning the Tour. Johan is simply part of my life. We talk to each other three or four times a day, whether it's June or January. We talk all the time. He's a fanatic, like me. . . . We adore what we do, we adore this sport, we adore this event, and we adore the team. We have lots of things in common; I can't imagine doing this without him.

Q: With four consecutive wins in the Tour de France, you have already made a mark in the history of cycling; what is the image, the impression that you would like to leave behind you?
LA: Whatever the number of victories, never before had the Tour been won by a "cancer survivor." For that, I will be remembered. As for the rest, I'm still active and I can't imagine what trace I will have left in ten, fifteen, fifty years. . . . We'll see.

It will be up to others, the journalists, the public to decide.

Q: What is your reaction to those who say that overcoming illness modified your body and your personality to the point of being able to win the Tour?
LA: It's true! I have always said it: Physically, mentally, emotionally, cancer has changed the athlete that I am, in a positive way. It was an inestimable experience and, paradoxically, a good thing for me.

Q: It's your fourth consecutive win; can you imagine the impact of a fifth win in 2003?
LA: I am very happy to have won, because it is for this goal that I devote all my time, all my energy, all my year. . . . Defeat would have profoundly disappointed me. Every year, the feeling is different. This is why I

am incapable of saying how I would feel about a fifth victory. As to the significance of such an event in the world of cycling and sport in general, I have no idea. Maybe I will next year. In the meantime, I live for the present.

Q: Are you going to turn the page at the end of the day on July 28, toward joining your wife and your children?
LA: I have no idea. . . . When the Tour is finished, we close the book and the pressure goes away. But you know, I love this race and I savor it a little more each year. I reflect on the key moments of the season, during the preparation, then after the Tour, the warm summer and the satisfaction as much as the inner peace that I feel. You know, what I like most of all is to come to France, hoping to win and, eventually, winning!

The stages

saturday, july 6th	**Prologue** — Luxembourg —	**7 km**
sunday, july 7th	**stage 1** — Luxembourg > Luxembourg —	**192.5 km**
monday, july 8th	**stage 2** — Luxembourg > Sarrebruck —	**181 km**
tuesday, july 9th	**stage 3** — Metz > Reims —	**174.5 km**
wednesday, july 10th	**stage 4** — Épernay > Château-Thierry —	**67.5 km**
thursday, july 11th	**stage 5** — Soissons > Rouen —	**195 km**
friday, july 12th	**stage 6** — Forges-les-Eaux > Alençon —	**199.5 km**
saturday, july 13th	**stage 7** — Bagnoles-de-l'Orme > Avranches —	**174.5 km**
sunday, july 14th	**stage 8** — Saint-Martin-de-Landelles > Plouay —	**217.5 km**
monday, july 15th	**stage 9** — Lanester > Lorient —	**52 km**
wednesday, july 17th	**stage 10** — Bazas > Pau —	**147 km**
thursday, july 18th	**stage 11** — Pau > La Mongie —	**158 km**
friday, july 19th	**stage 12** — Lannemezan > Plateau de Beille —	**199.5 km**
saturday, july 20th	**stage 13** — Lavelanet > Béziers —	**171 km**
sunday, july 21st	**stage 14** — Lodève > Mont Ventoux —	**221 km**
tuesday, july 23rd	**stage 15** — Vaison-La-Romaine > Les Deux-Alpes —	**226.5 km**
wednesday, july 24th	**stage 16** — Les Deux-Alpes > La Plagne —	**179.5 km**
thursday, july 25th	**stage 17** — Aime > Cluses —	**142 km**
friday, july 26th	**stage 18** — Cluses > Bourg-en-Bresse —	**176.5 km**
saturday, july 27th	**stage 19** — Régnié-Durette > Mâcon —	**50 km**
sunday, july 28th	**stage 20** — Melun > Paris-Champs-Élysées —	**144 km**

DAY AFTER DAY

saturday, july 6th **Prologue** — Luxembourg — **7 km**

ARMSTRONG AS USUAL

When the fluidity of the rider and the talents of the photographer join forces (Lance Armstrong and Jean-Christophe Moreau), the picture captures the glory of cycling.

Three-time champion Armstrong delivered a touch of déjà vu by starting the Tour de France with a victory. A wet start to the day threatened to add an element of danger to the prologue of the 89th Tour de France, but once the riders began their race against the clock in the twisting, partially cobbled, and rolling course, the rain ceased and the roads dried. Armstrong bolted from the starthouse at an average speed of 45.985 kph and raced down the smooth descents, through the cobbled back streets, out of the valley, and on through the finish to secure a predictable victory 2 seconds ahead of last year's two-time stage winner, Jalabert of France. Australia's McGee set the fastest pace at the 3.5 km mark and held the lead momentarily. Then came a charge from the lone Hungarian in the race, Bodrogi who edged out McGee by a fraction of a second. Following Bodrogi was a selection of riders from the thirty nations represented: Spain (with Gonzalez de Galdeano), Italy (Frigo), Britain (Millar), Colombia (Botero), and Lithuania (Rumsas). Nine countries and three continents were represented in the top eleven finishers, a Tour record.

PROLOGUE RESULTS

1. Lance ARMSTRONG (USA), U.S. Postal	9:08
2. Laurent JALABERT (F), CSC-Tiscali	+ 0:02
3. Raimondas RUMSAS (Lit), Lampre	+ 0:03
4. Santiago BOTERO (Col), Kelme	+ 0:04
5. David MILLAR (GB), Cofidis	+ 0:05

Green Jersey Lance ARMSTRONG (USA), U.S. Postal		15 pts
White Jersey David MILLAR (GB), Cofidis		09:13
Team Classification CSC-TISCALI		27:58

GENERAL CLASSIFICATION

1. Lance ARMSTRONG (USA), U.S. Postal	09:08
2. Laurent JALABERT (F), CSC-Tiscali	+ 0:02
3. Raimondas RUMSAS (Lit), Lampre	+ 0:03
4. Santiago BOTERO (Col), Kelme	+ 0:04
5. David MILLAR (GB), Cofidis	+ 0:05

Green Jersey Lance ARMSTRONG (USA), U.S. Postal	15 pts
White Jersey David MILLAR (GB), Cofidis	09:13
Team Classification CSC-TISCALI	27:58

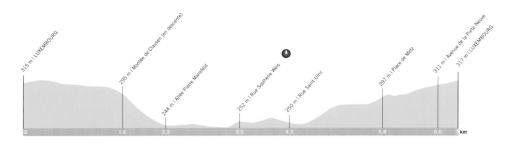

sunday, july 7th **stage 1** — Luxembourg > Luxembourg — **192.5 km**

THE KING!

Bertogliati embodies the words of Rodrigo in El Cid: "I am young it is true; but for souls of noble birth, merit does not depend on the number of years."

The first stage began at 12:45 p.m. with 189 riders. The first hour of racing saw no attacks and an average speed of 33.1 kph. The first sprint was won by Zabel, ahead of O'Grady and Jalabert, who was the virtual leader after finishing the prologue less than 2 seconds behind Armstrong. Bergès began the first successful break at the 53 km mark. He was joined by Dierckxsens and Mengin. Their lead grew to 1:05 at the 60 km mark and the leading trio pushed its advantage to a maximum of 4:05 as the peloton passed through the feed zone. The third climb really set the race alight. Mengin dropped his escape companions and the peloton was attacked by McGee and Halgand. Serpellini then attacked and was joined by Moreni, Lefèvre, and Casar with 26 km to race. Their lead on the peloton with 24 km to go was 45 seconds. Lefèvre attacked the lead group on the final climb. The peloton caught the other three before the summit. The peloton reformed with 3.5 km to go. Telekom riders led up until the final kilometer when Bertogliati surged ahead to take his first Tour de France stage win in his second start. His nineteenth place finish in the prologue (17 seconds behind Armstrong) was enough to allow him to take the 20 second time bonus and the overall lead.

STAGE 1 RESULTS

1. Rubens BERTOGLIATI (Swi), Lampre	4:49:16
2. Erik ZABEL (G), Telekom	s.t.
3. Robbie McEWEN (Aus), Lotto	s.t.
4. Fabio BALDATO (I), Fassa	s.t.
5. Oscar FREIRE (Sp), Mapei	s.t.

Green Jersey Erik ZABEL (G), Telekom	36 pts
Polka-dot Jersey Christophe MENGIN (F), FDJeux.com	22 pts
White Jersey Rubens BERTOGLIATI (Swi), Lampre	4:49:16
Team Classification KELME	14:27:48
Most Aggressive Rider Stéphane BERGÈS (F), AG2R	12 pts

GENERAL CLASSIFICATION

1. Rubens BERTOGLIATI (Swi), Lampre	4:58:21
2. Laurent JALABERT (F), CSC-Tiscali	+ 0:03
3. Lance ARMSTRONG (USA), U.S. Postal	+ 0:03
4. Raimondas RUMSAS (Lit), Lampre	+ 0:06
5. Santiago BOTERO (Col), Kelme	+ 0:07

Green Jersey Erik ZABEL (G), Telekom	36 pts
Polka-dot Jersey Christophe MENGIN (F), FDJeux.com	22 pts
White Jersey Rubens BERTOGLIATI (Swi), Lampre	4:58:21
Team Classification CSC-TISCALI	14:55:46
Most Aggressive Rider Stéphane BERGÈS (F), AG2R	12 pts

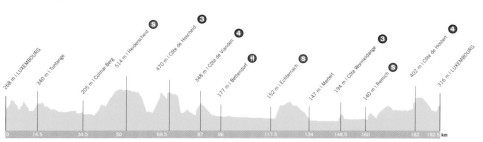

stage 2 — Luxembourg > Sarrebruck — **181 km**

FREIRE'S RAINBOW

Unhappy on his arrival in Luxembourg, the Spanish world champion Oscar Freire didn't take long to get his reflexes back: position, outflank, and win!

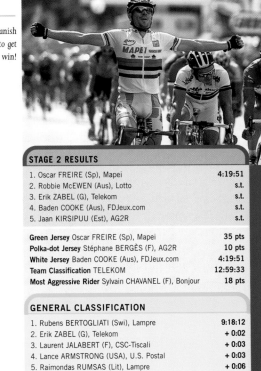

The 181-km second stage began at 12:41 p.m. with 189 riders. The forecast for the day was for 86° Fahrenheit. The first attack of the day came from Chavanel at the 11 km mark. He was chased down by Hushovd and Bergès. At the 20 km mark, they had a lead of 42 seconds. The Lampre team of the overall leader, Bertogliati, led the peloton. As they raced into Germany, the leading trio's advantage was 3:45. With 98 km to race, the trio's lead reached a maximum of 5:05. At the 113 km mark, Hushovd dropped out of the lead group with a cramp: The peloton caught him on the approach to the day's second climb, where he was dropped. With 31 km to go, Hoshovd's teammate Jens Voigt, a German, attacked the peloton. He quickly caught the two remaining escapees. With 27 km to go, the three were 53 seconds ahead of the peloton. With 16 km to go, Voigt was all alone, but he was quickly caught. His teammate Hinault attacked, but without success. The Telekom riders did all they could to lead home the local boy, Zabel, for the win and they controlled the peloton until the last 500 m. McEwen began the sprint with about 350 m to go and moved ahead of Zabel, but world champion Oscar Freire passed the Australian champion in the final meters to win by about one bike length.

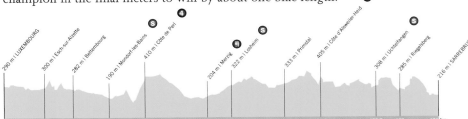

STAGE 2 RESULTS

1. Oscar FREIRE (Sp), Mapei	4:19:51
2. Robbie McEWEN (Aus), Lotto	s.t.
3. Erik ZABEL (G), Telekom	s.t.
4. Baden COOKE (Aus), FDJeux.com	s.t.
5. Jaan KIRSIPUU (Est), AG2R	s.t.

Green Jersey Oscar FREIRE (Sp), Mapei	35 pts
Polka-dot Jersey Stéphane BERGÈS (F), AG2R	10 pts
White Jersey Baden COOKE (Aus), FDJeux.com	4:19:51
Team Classification TELEKOM	12:59:33
Most Aggressive Rider Sylvain CHAVANEL (F), Bonjour	18 pts

GENERAL CLASSIFICATION

1. Rubens BERTOGLIATI (Swi), Lampre	9:18:12
2. Erik ZABEL (G), Telekom	+ 0:02
3. Laurent JALABERT (F), CSC-Tiscali	+ 0:03
4. Lance ARMSTRONG (USA), U.S. Postal	+ 0:03
5. Raimondas RUMSAS (Lit), Lampre	+ 0:06

Green Jersey Erik ZABEL (G), Telekom	62 pts
Polka-dot Jersey Stéphane BERGÈS (F), AG2R	26 pts
White Jersey Rubens BERTOGLIATI (Swi), Lampre	9:18:12
Team Classification CSC-TISCALI	27:55:19
Most Aggressive Rider Stéphane BERGÈS (F), AG2R	24 pts

---

stage 3 — Metz > Reims — **174.5 km**

GREEN AND YELLOW

An exceptional year for Robbie McEwen, who, since his national champion title continues to rack up wins. Following O'Grady in 2001, McEwen is a new Australian rival for Erik Zabel.

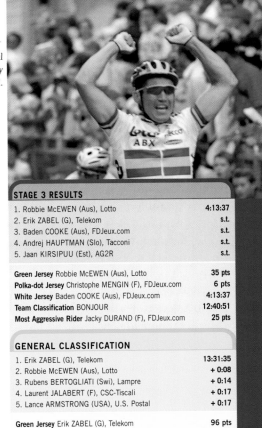

The 174.5-km third stage began at 12:59 p.m. with 189 riders still in the race. At the summit of the Côte de Gravelotte, Mengin raced up the early climb to muscle his way back into the virtual lead of the polka-dot jersey classification. At the 6 km mark, Durand attacked and was joined by Rénier. Together they pushed their advantage to 1:25 at the 14 km mark. Their advantage reached a maximum at the 68 km mark when they were 11:10 ahead of the peloton. At this point, the Lotto team joined Telekom at the front of the peloton. With 85 km to go, the lead had dropped to 7:10. At the second intermediate sprint, the points were won by Durand, ahead of Renier and Zabel, whose 2 second time bonus put him on equal time as Bertogliati. At the Suippes sprint, Zabel, third, simply rolled through to take the time bonus and push his way past Bertogliati in the GC. With 30 km to race, the leading pair was 3:05 ahead of the peloton. They were caught with 8.5 km left to race. Bertogliati moved to the front with 5 km to go, but was swallowed up by the sprinters' teams. Robbie McEwen, wearing the green and yellow Australian champion's jersey, captured his second Tour de France stage win. In the green jersey, Erik Zabel's second place finish was enough to ensure that he started the fourth stage in yellow.

STAGE 3 RESULTS

1. Robbie McEWEN (Aus), Lotto	4:13:37
2. Erik ZABEL (G), Telekom	s.t.
3. Baden COOKE (Aus), FDJeux.com	s.t.
4. Andrej HAUPTMAN (Slo), Tacconi	s.t.
5. Jaan KIRSIPUU (Est), AG2R	s.t.

Green Jersey Robbie McEWEN (Aus), Lotto	35 pts
Polka-dot Jersey Christophe MENGIN (F), FDJeux.com	6 pts
White Jersey Baden COOKE (Aus), FDJeux.com	4:13:37
Team Classification BONJOUR	12:40:51
Most Aggressive Rider Jacky DURAND (F), FDJeux.com	25 pts

GENERAL CLASSIFICATION

1. Erik ZABEL (G), Telekom	13:31:35
2. Robbie McEWEN (Aus), Lotto	+ 0:08
3. Rubens BERTOGLIATI (Swi), Lampre	+ 0:14
4. Laurent JALABERT (F), CSC-Tiscali	+ 0:17
5. Lance ARMSTRONG (USA), U.S. Postal	+ 0:17

Green Jersey Erik ZABEL (G), Telekom	96 pts
Polka-dot Jersey Christophe MENGIN (F), FDJeux.com	29 pts
White Jersey Rubens BERTOGLIATI (Swi), Lampre	13:31:49
Team Classification CSC-TISCALI	40:36:10
Most Aggressive Rider Jacky DURAND (F), FDJeux.com	25 pts

ONCE AGAIN!

In yellow in the race, in pink on the podium, the Spanish team ONCE-Eroski indeed sees life through rose and yellow colored glasses. Stage victory and first place in the overall classification—felicidades!

Igor Gonzalez de Galdeano finished last year's Tour in fifth place overall. It was a good result for the Spanish ONCE-Eroski rider with a proven pedigree, but after the fourth stage of this year's tour, he donned the race's yellow jersey to further confirm his overall talents. ONCE took the win 16 seconds ahead of the U.S. Postal Service team and 46 seconds in front of the CSC-Tiscali formation. Eight of ONCE's nine riders found themselves in the top twelve overall. The U.S. Postal team had eight riders in the top twenty. Perhaps it was the lure of grandeur that prompted CSC-Tiscali to make one small faux-pas in this stage, which it was dominating until the Danish champion, Michael Sandstödt, punctured after the 40.5 km time check in Breuil. Until then, the Danish-registered team was in control. It led ONCE by 6 seconds at the 21.5 and the 40.5 km checks, but then opted to wait for Sandstöd until it became apparent that he couldn't rejoin the crew of Jalabert and Hamilton. Before that error, it seemed inevitable that Jalabert would make the jump from fourth to first overall—just as he'd done when riding with the ONCE team back in 2000 when they won the team time trial in St. Nazaire. But because of their pause, Jalabert was pushed back to fifteenth overall—the only "hiccup" in a top twenty full of only ONCE and Postal riders.

STAGE 4 RESULTS

1. ONCE	1:19:49
2. U.S. POSTAL	+ 0:16
3. CSC-TISCALI	+ 0:46
4. FASSA	+ 1:30
5. COFIDIS	+ 1:44

Team Classification ONCE	3:59:27

GENERAL CLASSIFICATION

1. Igor GONZALEZ DE GALDEANO (Sp), ONCE	14:51:50
2. Joseba BELOKI (Sp), ONCE	+ 0:04
3. Lance ARMSTRONG (USA), U.S. Postal	+ 0:07
4. Jorg JAKSCHE (G), ONCE	+ 0:12
5. Abraham OLANO (Sp), ONCE	+ 0:22

Green Jersey Erik ZABEL (G), Telekom	96 pts
Polka-dot Jersey Christophe MENGIN (F), FDJeux.com	29 pts
White Jersey Isidro NOZAL (Sp), ONCE	14:52:17
Team Classification ONCE	44:35:46
Most Aggressive Rider Jacky DURAND (F), FDJeux.com	25 pts

THE BALTIC SPRINTER

It is sometimes easier to win a pack sprint than a five-rider finish. The redoubtable Estonian sprinter Jaan Kirsipuu attacked from all angles in the finale and managed things brilliantly.

The 195-km fifth stage began at 12:39 p.m. with 189 riders still in the race. The numerous attacks at the start of the stage yielded an average speed for the first hour of 48.7 kph! ONCE and Telekom led the peloton's chase of all escapees. At the 73 km mark, an attack of seventeen riders went clear. This group reached a maximum lead of 35 seconds but was caught with 100 km to go. At this stage, Tom Steels became the first rider to abandon the 89th Tour de France. Kirsipuu, Sandstöd, Dierckxsens, Casagrande, and Edaleine attacked with 85 km to race. Within 5 km, they had a lead of 1 minute. With 46 km to go, Edaleine became the third virtual leader of the day when his group pushed its lead to 4:50—its maximum advantage. The Lotto team then began working at the front of the peloton. With 25 km to go, the five leaders were 3 minutes ahead of the peloton being led by Crédit Agricole, Lotto, and FDJeux.com. The five riders held off the peloton (by 33 seconds). They worked well together until the final kilometer when Sandstöd launched the first attack. Then Dierckxsens tried his luck. Kirsipuu covered all the moves and eventually sprinted for the win over the Dane and the Belgian.

STAGE 5 RESULTS

1. Jaan KIRSIPUU (Est), AG2R	4:13:33
2. Michael SANDSTÖD (Dk), CSC-Tiscali	s.t.
3. Ludo DIERCKXSENS (Bel), Lampre	s.t.
4. Stefano CASAGRANDA (I), Alessio	+ 0:03
5. Christophe EDALEINE (F), Delatour	+ 0:08

Green Jersey Michael SANDSTÖD (Dk), CSC-Tiscali	40 pts
White Jersey Christophe EDALEINE (F), Delatour	4:13:33
Team Classification LAMPRE	12:41:45
Most Aggressive Rider Stefano CASAGRANDA (I), Alessio	14 pts

GENERAL CLASSIFICATION

1. Igor GONZALEZ DE GALDEANO (Sp), ONCE	19:05:56
2. Joseba BELOKI (Sp), ONCE	+ 0:04
3. Lance ARMSTRONG (USA), U.S. Postal	+ 0:07
4. Jörg JAKSCHE (G), ONCE	+ 0:12
5. Abraham OLANO (Sp), ONCE	+ 0:22

Green Jersey Erik ZABEL (G), Telekom	113 pts
Polka-dot Jersey Christophe MENGIN (F), FDJeux.com	29 pts
White Jersey Isidro NOZAL (Sp), ONCE	19:06:23
Team Classification ONCE	57:18:04
Most Aggressive Rider Jacky DURAND (F), FDJeux.com	25 pts

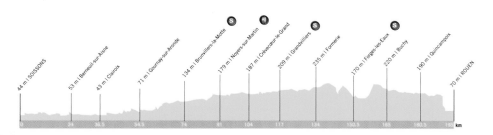

stage 6 — Forges-les-Eaux > Alençon — **199.5 km**

ZABEL SEES GREEN

Despite a stage win, the German Erik Zabel eventually failed in his attempt to win a seventh green jersey in the 2002 Tour.

The 199.5-km sixth stage began at 12:31 p.m. with 186 riders—Verbrugghe did not take the start. After many attacks, McEwen took the virtual lead in the sprint classification at the first intermediate sprint. The average speed for the first 2 hours was 43.65 kph. After the feed zone, the peloton was attacked by numerous riders from just about every team (except ONCE and U.S. Postal). Eventually, a group of six riders—Wesemann, Zaballa, van Hyfte, Durand, Magnien, and Apollonio—managed to break free. At the 125 km mark, they were 1:40 ahead. Then Lotto and ONCE agreed to share the chase. Just before the second sprint, the lead group was 1:45 ahead. With 55 km to go, the lead was down to 1:20. The Lotto and ONCE teams were joined by Mapei and Crédit Agricole at the front of the peloton. With 30 km to go, the peloton was 40 seconds behind. Durand tried one last effort 11 km from the line as the others were caught by the peloton. The Frenchman was eventually caught as he reached the 10 km banner. The final 10 km were controlled by the Mapei, Lotto, Crédit Agricole, and Telekom teams. Hondo led into the final turn and his leader, the green-clad Erik Zabel, finished the job to take the win.

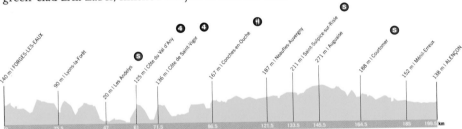

STAGE 6 RESULTS

1. Erik ZABEL (G), Telekom	4:19:51
2. Oscar FREIRE (Sp), Mapei	s.t.
3. Robbie McEWEN (Aus), Lotto	s.t.
4. Jan SVORADA (Cz), Lampre	s.t.
5. Sergeï IVANOV (Rus), Fassa	s.t.

Green Jersey Erik ZABEL (G), Telekom	37 pts
Polka-dot Jersey Christophe MENGIN (F), FDJeux.com	10 pts
White Jersey Baden COOKE (Aus), FDJeux.com	4:23:07
Team Classification TACCONI	13:09:21
Most Aggressive Rider Steffen WESEMANN (G), Telekom	9 pts

GENERAL CLASSIFICATION

1. Igor GONZALEZ DE GALDEANO (Sp), ONCE	23:29:03
2. Joseba BELOKI (Sp), ONCE	+ 0:04
3. Lance ARMSTRONG (USA), U.S. Postal	+ 0:07
4. Jörg JAKSCHE (G), ONCE	+ 0:12
5. Abraham OLANO (Sp), ONCE	+ 0:22

Green Jersey Erik ZABEL (G), Telekom	150 pts
Polka-dot Jersey Christophe MENGIN (F), FDJeux.com	39 pts
White Jersey Isidro NOZAL (Sp), ONCE	23:29:30
Team Classification ONCE	70:27:25
Most Aggressive Rider Jacky DURAND (F), FDJeux.com	32 pts

---

stage 7 — Bagnoles-de-l'Orne > Avranches — **174.5 km**

McGEE'S STAGE WIN

Australia is a breeding ground for cycling champions: In recruiting Bradley McGee, visibly hungry for victory, FDJeux.com team director Marc Madiot proved that he has flair.

The 176-km seventh stage began at 1:01 p.m. with 185 riders in the race (one rider missing: Alexandr Shefer). After Chavanel escaped, his teammate Renier was the next to attack (at the 22 km mark). He was joined by Van Bon and Morin. At the first sprint, the peloton was behind by 25 seconds. At the 40 km mark, the trio led by 1:30. At this stage, the leading trio was 2:20 ahead of the peloton. At the 49 km mark, the trio led by 3 minutes. The biggest lead of the day was at the 92 km mark, when the peloton was behind by 5:20. With 50 km to race, the leading trio was 3:15 ahead of the peloton. With 10 km to go the lead diminished to 45 seconds. The escape was caught 3 km before the finish. There was a fall at the 173 km mark with Freire and Moreau involved, and Rous was taken away in an ambulance. With 2 km to go, Armstrong and Jalabert were delayed by another fall. They quickly started chasing and finished 26 seconds behind the stage winner. With about 1,100 m to go, Pedro Horrillo attacked. He led for the final kilometer, chased all the way by McGee, who passed him just before the line to take his first stage win in the Tour.

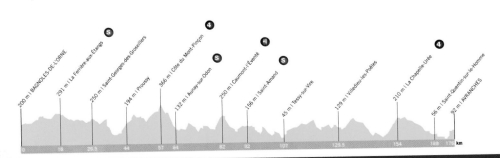

STAGE 7 RESULTS

1. Bradley McGEE (Aus), FDJeux.com	4:10:56
2. Jaan KIRSIPUU (Est), AG2R	s.t.
3. Pedro HORRILLO (Sp), Mapei	s.t.
4. Robbie McEWEN (Aus), Lotto	s.t.
5. Erik ZABEL (G), Telekom	s.t.

Green Jersey Bradley McGEE (Aus), FDJeux.com	35 pts
Polka-dot Jersey Anthony MORIN (F), Crédit Agricole	8 pts
White Jersey Baden COOKE (Aus), FDJeux.com	4:10:56
Team Classification FDJEUX.COM	12:32:48
Most Aggressive Rider Franck RENIER (F), Bonjour	18 pts

GENERAL CLASSIFICATION

1. Igor GONZALEZ DE GALDEANO (Sp), ONCE	27:39:59
2. Joseba BELOKI (Sp), ONCE	+ 0:04
3. Jörg JAKSCHE (G), ONCE	+ 0:12
4. Abraham OLANO (Sp), ONCE	+ 0:22
5. Isidro NOZAL (Sp), ONCE	+ 0:27

Green Jersey Erik ZABEL (G), Telekom	172 pts
Polka-dot Jersey Christophe MENGIN (F), FDJeux.com	39 pts
White Jersey Isidro NOZAL (Sp), ONCE	27:40:26
Team Classification ONCE	83:00:13
Most Aggressive Rider Franck RENIER (F), Bonjour	38 pts

KROON WINS PLOUAY

Karsten Kroon can't believe what he sees—he has to take off his glasses to witness his first stage victory in the Tour de France.

The 217.5-km eighth stage began at 12:01 p.m. There were 182 riders at the start. Two riders abandoned overnight—Freire (Mapei) and Vierhouten (Lotto). The average speed for the first hour was a rapid 48.9 kph! Padrnos, Tauler, Piziks, Rodriguez, Casar, Bouyer, Chavanel, Pineau, De Waele, Turpin, Halgand, and Moreni attacked at the 81 km mark. This escape was caught by the peloton at the 100 km mark. The average speed for the second hour was 49.7 kph! At the 108 km mark, Hinault (Crédit Agricole), Knaven (Domo), Dekker and Kroon (Rabobank), Renier (Bonjour), Belohvosciks (Lampre), and Augé (Delatour) attacked. They pushed their advantage to 1 minute by the 115 km mark. At the 80 km mark, their lead was 4:05. Renier's group pushed its lead to 4:40 after 3 hours of racing. The maximum advantage of the break was 6 minutes with 66 km to race—then the AG2R team joined ONCE's chase at the front of the peloton. At the third sprint, the peloton was behind by 4:35. Each rider (except Karsten Kroon) attacked in the closing 5 km. After his teammate Dekker led out the sprint, Kroon raced through in the final meters to hold off the fast-finishing Knaven for his first Tour stage win. Robbie McEwen led home the peloton 1:55 later.

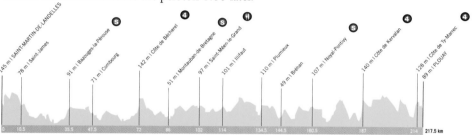

STAGE 8 RESULTS

1. Karsten KROON (Nl), Rabobank		4:36:52
2. Servais KNAVEN (Nl), Domo		s.t.
3. Erik DEKKER (Nl), Rabobank		s.t.
4. Franck RENIER (F), Bonjour		s.t.
5. Sébastien HINAULT (F), Crédit Agricole		s.t.

Green Jersey Karsten KROON (Nl), Rabobank	39 pts
Polka-dot Jersey Raivis BELOHVOSCIKS (Lat), Lampre	10 pts
White Jersey Baden COOKE (Aus), FDJeux.com	4:38:47
Team Classification RABOBANK	13:52:31
Most Aggressive Rider Raivis BELOHVOSCIKS (Lat), Lampre	12 pts

GENERAL CLASSIFICATION

1. Igor GONZALEZ DE GALDEANO (Sp), ONCE	32:18:46
2. Joseba BELOKI (Sp), ONCE	+ 0:04
3. Jörg JAKSCHE (G), ONCE	+ 0:12
4. Abraham OLANO (Sp), ONCE	+ 0:22
5. Isidro NOZAL (Sp), ONCE	+ 0:27

Green Jersey Erik ZABEL (G), Telekom	193 pts
Polka-dot Jersey Christophe MENGIN (F), FDJeux.com	42 pts
White Jersey Isidro NOZAL (Sp), ONCE	32:19:13
Team Classification ONCE	96:56:54
Most Aggressive Rider Franck RENIER (F), Bonjour	49 pts

BOTERO FIRES FIRST SHOT

Bubbly Coca-Cola to celebrate the historic victory of Santiago Botero—the first Colombian to win a Tour de France time trial.

So much can happen in 52 km—especially when the only thing a rider can count on to carry him to the finish line is the strength of his own legs. And in Brittany, Santiago Botero's legs were the most powerful of an elite group. The Colombian star didn't outwit his opponents to claim his second Tour stage win (a contrast to the manner in which he claimed the stage to Briançon two years ago). Racing along at an average speed of 50.08 kph, Botero beat the man who had won the overall title for the past three years. Armstrong didn't perform badly, but he didn't win the pre-mountain time trial as he did when there was such a challenge in 1999. He finished second, by a small margin of just 11 seconds—not a lot of time and good enough to push his ranking up to second overall—a small reminder that he is indeed human. Armstrong also failed to take the yellow jersey from Igor Gonzalez de Galdeano, who continued to wear the golden glow of the overall leader after a great race to finish the stage in fourth, only 8 seconds behind the U.S. Postal leader. However, French contenders (Jalabert—victim of a puncture, Virenque, Moreau . . .) lost too much time and their hopes of climbing on the podium in Paris faded. In the end it was Botero—the surprise of 2000—who fired the first shots in the battle for overall glory.

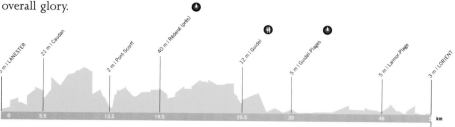

STAGE 9 RESULTS

1. Santiago BOTERO (Col), Kelme	1:02:18
2. Lance ARMSTRONG (USA), U.S. Postal	+ 0:11
3. Serhiy HONCHAR (Ukr), Fassa	+ 0:18
4. Igor GONZALEZ DE GALDEANO (Sp), ONCE	+ 0:19
5. Laszlo BODROGI (Hun), Mapei	+ 0:25

Green Jersey Santiago BOTERO (Col), Kelme	15 pts
White Jersey David MILLAR (GB), Cofidis	1:03:08
Team Classification U.S. POSTAL	3:11:07

GENERAL CLASSIFICATION

1. Igor GONZALEZ DE GALDEANO (Sp), ONCE	33:21:23
2. Lance ARMSTRONG (USA), U.S. Postal	+ 0:26
3. Joseba BELOKI (Sp), ONCE	+ 1:23
4. Serhiy HONCHAR (Ukr), Fassa	+ 1:35
5. Santiago BOTERO (Col), Kelme	+ 1:55

Green Jersey Erik ZABEL (G), Telekom	193 pts
Polka-dot Jersey Christophe MENGIN (F), FDJeux.com	42 pts
White Jersey David MILLAR (GB), Cofidis	33:23:34
Team Classification ONCE	100:08:01
Most Aggressive Rider Franck RENIER (F), Bonjour	49 pts

stage 10 — Bazas > Pau — **147 km**

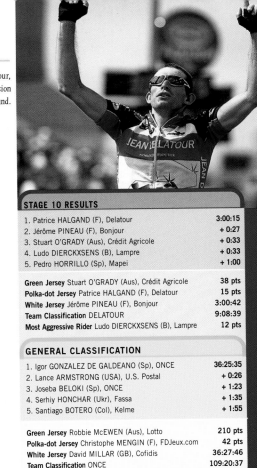

The last team selected to participate in the Tour, Jean Delatour, had to win a stage: Mission accomplished with Patrice Halgand.

A VICTORY FOR FRANCE

The 147-km stage from Bazas to Pau started at 2:05 p.m. with 182 riders. The pack was still together after one hour of racing—at an average speed of 54.5 kph! With 77 km to race, a break-away group of 11 riders formed and within 70 km pushed its advantage to 1:25. The group included Mattan (Cofidis), O'Grady (Crédit Agricole), Cassani (Domo), Horillo (Mapei), Flickinger (AG2R), Zaballa (Kelme), Vogondy (FDJeux.com), Pineau (Bonjour), Dierckxsens (Lampre), Unai Etxebarria (Euskaltel), and Halgand (Delatour). After two hours of racing, the average speed was 52.1 kph. With 40 km to race, the eleven led the peloton by 3:03. At the last summit a surge by Halgand dropped Etxebarria and a lead group of four formed: Halgand, O'Grady, Dierckxsens, and Pineau. With 15 km to go, they were 30 seconds ahead of the other six (Etxebarria dropped out of the lead group on the Côte d'Auga); the peloton was 4:02 behind. Halgand attacked with 7.5 km to go and the Delatour rider eventually won the stage at an average speed of 48.9 kph. Cooke led home the main pack 3:57 behind Halgand. McEwen was thirteenth—and took enough points to inherit the green jersey of best sprinter.

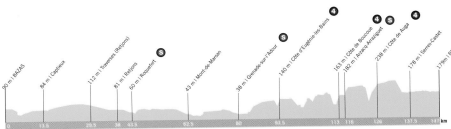

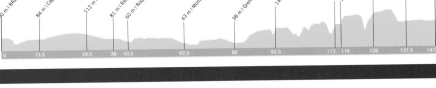

STAGE 10 RESULTS

1. Patrice HALGAND (F), Delatour		3:00:15
2. Jérôme PINEAU (F), Bonjour		+ 0:27
3. Stuart O'GRADY (Aus), Crédit Agricole		+ 0:33
4. Ludo DIERCKXSENS (B), Lampre		+ 0:33
5. Pedro HORRILLO (Sp), Mapei		+ 1:00

Green Jersey Stuart O'GRADY (Aus), Crédit Agricole		38 pts
Polka-dot Jersey Patrice HALGAND (F), Delatour		15 pts
White Jersey Jérôme PINEAU (F), Bonjour		3:00:42
Team Classification DELATOUR		9:08:39
Most Aggressive Rider Ludo DIERCKXSENS (B), Lampre		12 pts

GENERAL CLASSIFICATION

1. Igor GONZALEZ DE GALDEANO (Sp), ONCE		36:25:35
2. Lance ARMSTRONG (USA), U.S. Postal		+ 0:26
3. Joseba BELOKI (Sp), ONCE		+ 1:23
4. Serhiy HONCHAR (Ukr), Fassa		+ 1:35
5. Santiago BOTERO (Col), Kelme		+ 1:55

Green Jersey Robbie McEWEN (Aus), Lotto		210 pts
Polka-dot Jersey Christophe MENGIN (F), FDJeux.com		42 pts
White Jersey David MILLAR (GB), Cofidis		36:27:46
Team Classification ONCE		109:20:37
Most Aggressive Rider Franck RENIER (F), Bonjour		50 pts

---

stage 11 — Pau > La Mongie — **158 km**

LANCE BREAKS THE SUSPENSE

Since 1999, it has become an habit: Lance Armstrong wins the first mountain stage of the Tour de France and takes the yellow jersey.

The 158-km eleventh stage from Pau to La Mongie began at 12:27 p.m. There were 181 riders in the race. With 125 km to go, Magnien attacked. With 120 km to race, he led a group of eight—Zaballa, Cuesta, Jalabert, Voigt, Bodrogi, Horrillo, D. Etxebarria, and Turpin—by 20 seconds and the peloton by 50 seconds. With 115 km to go, Magnien was caught by Jalabert's group. In the ascent of the Col d'Aubisque, Jalabert outdistanced the other escapees. At the summit of the Col du Soulor, Jalabert led McGee and Etxebarria by 1:30 and the peloton of Armstrong and the yellow jersey by 2:40. With 50 km to go, Jalabert's advantage grew to 3:55—his maximum lead in the stage. At the second sprint, Zabel's 4 points put him back in the lead of the sprint classification by 1 point. In the last climb, the U.S. Postal team raced with clever tactics as Hincapie set the pace early, then Rubiera. Then Heras came to the front with a little more than 5 km to race. Heras's surge was enough to discourage the challengers chasing Jalabert (with the exception of Armstrong and Beloki). Heras led the chase of Jalabert and the trio passed the Frenchman with just 3 km to go. Heras set the pace right through to the final 150 m when Armstrong surged forward to take the stage and the yellow jersey 7 seconds ahead of Beloki and 13 seconds ahead of Heras.

STAGE 11 RESULTS

1. Lance ARMSTRONG (USA), U.S. Postal		4:21:57
2. Joseba BELOKI (Sp), ONCE		+ 0:07
3. Roberto HERAS (Sp), U.S. Postal		+ 0:13
4. Francisco MANCEBO (Sp), iBanesto.com		+ 1:16
5. Raimondas RUMSAS (Lit), Lampre		+ 1:16

Green Jersey Lance ARMSTRONG (USA), U.S. Postal		20 pts
Polka-dot Jersey Laurent JALABERT (F), CSC-Tiscali		46 pts
White Jersey Ivan BASSO (I), Fassa		4:23:20
Team Classification ONCE		13:09:44
Most Aggressive Rider Jacky DURAND (F), FDJeux.com		25 pts

GENERAL CLASSIFICATION

1. Lance ARMSTRONG (USA), U.S. Postal		40:47:38
2. Joseba BELOKI (Sp), ONCE		+ 1:12
3. Igor GONZALEZ DE GALDEANO (Sp), ONCE		+ 1:48
4. Raimondas RUMSAS (Lit), Lampre		+ 3:32
5. Santiago BOTERO (Col), Kelme		+ 4:13

Green Jersey Erik ZABEL (G), Telekom		213 pts
Polka-dot Jersey Patrice HALGAND (F), Delatour		57 pts
White Jersey Ivan BASSO (I), Fassa		40:53:00
Team Classification ONCE		122:30:21
Most Aggressive Rider Franck RENIER (F), Bonjour		50 pts

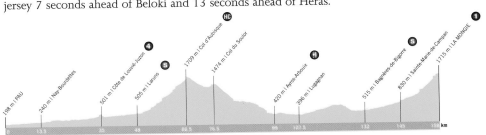

A REPEAT PERFORMANCE

The second stage in the Pyrénées is a repeat of the first: a breakaway from Jalabert and a comeback from Armstrong, who glues Beloki to the spot.

The twelfth stage officially began at 10:59 a.m. There were 176 riders at the start. The overnight withdrawal was the lone Brazillian in the Tour, Pagliarini.

Col de Mente & Col de Portet d'Aspet

Virenque was the first rider to attack. The average speed for the first hour was 36.5 kph. Virenque's escape was caught with 160 km to go. With 9.5 km to race to the first summit, Virenque, Jalabert, and Halgand attacked the peloton. They were 2:25 behind Oriol. With 6 km to climb, Oriol led Jalabert by 1:12 and a group of eleven by 1:30. At the summit of the Col de Mente, Oriol, Jalabert and Mazzoleni found themselves 2:10 ahead of the peloton. On the second climb, Oriol was caught and dropped by Jalabert.

Col de la Core

On the third climb, Oriol dropped out of the chase group. He was caught by the peloton with 100 km to race. At the mid-way mark, Jalabert, Nozal and Dufaux led Virenque's group by 2:35 and the peloton by 4:15. Virenque then surged and dropped Etxebarria, Zberg and Martinez. With 3 km to race, Jalabert's group led Virenque, Botcharov and Mazzoleni by 2:20 and the peloton by 3:30. At the summit, the results were: 1. Jalabert; 2. Dufaux; 3. Nozal; Virenque at 2:45; Mazzoleni and Botcharov at 2:48. Martinez was between the peloton (which was 4:10 behind and led over by Sevilla). Martinez rejoined Virenque's group on the descent. The maximum gain of Jalabert's group on the peloton was 5:40 (after 93 km). Virenque, Martinez, and Botcharov were caught 60 km from the finish. Mazzoleni attacked in the valley between the third and fourth climbs. He was caught by the peloton with 57 km to go. With 55 km to go, Jalabert's group led by 5:03.

Col de Port

There were no attacks on the fourth climb. Jalabert and Dufaux set the pace, Nozal followed and the U.S. Postal team led the peloton. At the summit, Jalabert led the race ahead of Dufaux, Nozal, and Virenque at 4:40. The next attack from Merckx and Konecny happened on the descent. With 30 km to race, Jalabert's group led this pair by 4:05 and the yellow jersey's peloton by 4:40. The Domo escapees were caught with 24 km to race. With 20 km to go, Lance's peloton was 3:40 behind the three leaders. All nine riders from the U.S. Postal team were at the front of this bunch. As the peloton arrived at the final climb, they were 2:45 behind.

The dance of Lance

As soon as the final climb began the U.S. Postal team thinned. Jalabert was caught with 9 km to race. Rubiera led until 8 km to go, then Heras took over. Heras's speed dropped the eight others who were still with the lead group. With 6 km to go, Lance attacked and raced on to take his fourteenth stage win in the Tour de France. Heras beat Beloki in the sprint for second place at 1:04. The U.S. Postal rider increased his overall lead and kept the yellow jersey. Laurent Jalabert finished 11:34 behind Armstrong, but having earned 96 pts from the stage, he inherited the polka-dot jersey.

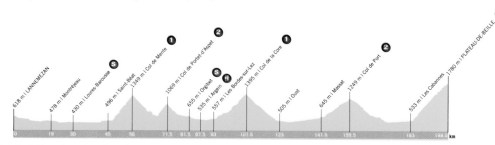

STAGE 12 RESULTS

1. Lance ARMSTRONG (USA), U.S. Postal	6:00:29
2. Roberto HERAS (Sp), U.S. Postal	+ 1:04
3. Joseba BELOKI (Sp), ONCE	+ 1:04
4. Santiago BOTERO (Col), Kelme	+ 1:11
5. Igor GONZALEZ DE GALDEANO (Sp), ONCE	+ 1:11
Green jersey Lance ARMSTRONG (USA), U.S. Postal	20 pts
Polka-dot Jersey Laurent JALABERT (F), CSC-Tiscali	96 pts
White Jersey Haimar ZUBELDIA (Sp), Euskaltel	6:04:50
Team Classification ONCE	8:05:19
Most Aggressive Rider Laurent JALABERT (F), CSC-Tiscali	30 pts

GENERAL CLASSIFICATION

1. Lance ARMSTRONG (USA), U.S. Postal	46:47:47
2. Joseba BELOKI (Sp), ONCE	+ 2:28
3. Igor GONZALEZ DE GALDEANO (Sp), ONCE	+ 3:19
4. Raimondas RUMSAS (Lit), Lampre	+ 5:15
5. Santiago BOTERO (Col), Kelme	+ 5:44
Green Jersey Erik ZABEL (G), Telekom	217 pts
Polka-dot Jersey Laurent JALABERT (F), CSC-Tiscali	142 pts
White Jersey Ivan BASSO (I), Fassa	47:00:16
Team Classification ONCE	140:35:40
Most Aggressive Rider Laurent JALABERT (F), CSC-Tiscali	75 pts

GLORY FOR SCOTLAND

Millar had declared before the start that he wanted to win this transition stage. Mission accomplished with authority and panache.

The 171-km thirteenth stage began at 1:17 p.m. There were 166 riders at the start. The non-starters were: Tauler, Hauptman, Casagranda, R. Ivanov, Pozzi, De Waele—all of whom abandoned during the twelfth stage. Simon, Sanchez, and Gonzalez finished outside the time limit. Durand was disqualified for holding onto a car on a climb of stage 12. Mazzoleni was the first to attack (at the 4 km mark). He was joined by Jalabert, Boogerd, and Millar. Then Julich, Zberg, Martinez, Latasa, Etxebarria, Brochard, and Pascual attacked the peloton. After 40 minutes of racing, the four led the seven by 54 seconds and the peloton by 3:35. With 119 km to go, the four leaders waited for the seven chasers. There were eleven riders in the lead at the 52 km mark (they were 8:05 ahead of the peloton). With 110 km to go, the peloton was behind by 7:24. With 20 km to go, the eleven-man escape group was 13 minutes ahead of the Lampre/Postal-led peloton. After Jalabert's attempt, Millar was the next to attack. His surge thinned the lead group down to five (Millar, Boogerd, Etxebarria, Pascual, and Brochard). In the closing 3 km there were attacks from all five riders in the lead group. The sprint was won by Millar.

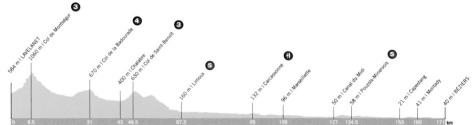

STAGE 13 RESULTS	
1. David MILLAR (GB), Cofidis	4:08:18
2. David ETXEBARRIA (Sp), Euskaltel	s.t.
3. Michaël BOOGERD (Nl), Rabobank	s.t.
4. Laurent BROCHARD (F), Delatour	s.t.
5. David LATASA (Sp), iBanesto.com	+ 0:04
Green Jersey David MILLAR (GB), Cofidis	35 pts
Polka-dot Jersey Laurent JALABERT (F), CSC-Tiscali	25 pts
White Jersey David MILLAR (GB), Cofidis	4:08:18
Team Classification iBANESTO.COM	12:35:50
Most Aggressive Rider Eddy MAZZOLENI (I), Tacconi	16 pts

GENERAL CLASSIFICATION	
1. Lance ARMSTRONG (USA), U.S. Postal	51:06:01
2. Joseba BELOKI (Sp), ONCE	+ 2:28
3. Igor GONZALEZ DE GALDEANO (Sp), ONCE	+ 3:19
4. Raimondas RUMSAS (Lit), Lampre	+ 5:15
5. Santiago BOTERO (Col), Kelme	+ 5:44
Green Jersey Robbie McEWEN (Aus), Lotto	229 pts
Polka-dot Jersey Laurent JALABERT (F), CSC-Tiscali	167 pts
White Jersey Ivan BASSO (I), Fassa	51:18:30
Team Classification ONCE	153:30:22
Most aggressive rider Laurent JALABERT (F), CSC-Tiscali	88 pts

D-DAY FOR VIRENQUE

By winning in the Mont Ventoux, Richard Virenque adds his name to the legend of the Tour.

The 221-km fourteenth stage from Lodeve to Mont Ventoux began at 11:22 a.m. There were 164 riders at the start—Gomez and Bossoni had abandoned during stage 13. At 21 km Pradera, Hushovd, Morin, Virenque, Velo, Baranowski, Serpellini, Botcharov, Moreni, Augé, and Edaleine attacked. At the 50 km mark, the eleven led the peloton by 9:45. The eleven-man escape group pushed their advantage to a maximum of 12:02. Rabobank then joined U.S. Postal at the front of the peloton's chase. As the leading group began the climb of the Ventoux, they had a lead of 8 minutes. Moreni was the first to attack. He took five riders (Virenque, Botcharov, Serpellini, Baranowski and Pradera) with him with 18 km to go. The peloton was behind by 7:10. The next to attack was Botcharov and he dropped Baranowski. Virenque attacked Botcharov with 11 km to go. Beloki's attack left just five in the yellow pack: Armstrong, Azevedo, Rumsas, and Basso. Then Beloki attacked again and that prompted Armstrong to begin his assault-proper of the Ventoux. The yellow jersey matched the attack and raced past Beloki and immediately distanced the Spaniard. Virenque continued with his efforts. With 5 km to go the time gaps were: Virenque 1:25 ahead of Botcharov; 2 minutes ahead of Serpellini; 3:15 ahead of Baranowski; 3:50 ahead of Armstrong, who could not fill the gap. Virenque won the stage ahead of Botcharov by 1:58 and 2:20 ahead of Armstrong.

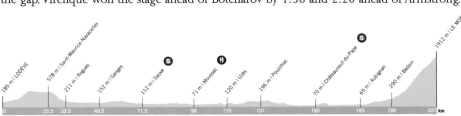

STAGE 14 RESUULTS	
1. Richard VIRENQUE (F), Domo	5:43:26
2. Alexandre BOTCHAROV (Rus), AG2R	+ 1:58
3. Lance ARMSTRONG (USA), U.S. Postal	+ 2:20
4. Marco SERPELLINI (I), Lampre	+ 2:54
5. Raimondas RUMSAS (Lit), Lampre	+ 3:36
Green Jersey Richard VIRENQUE (F), Domo	20 pts
Polka-dot Jersey Richard VIRENQUE (F), Domo	40 pts
White Jersey Ivan BASSO (I), Fassa	5:47:05
Team Classiification iBanesto.com	17:26:33
Most aggressive rider Alexandre BOTCHAROV (Rus), AG2R	12 pts

GENERAL CLASSIFICATION	
1. Lance ARMSTRONG (USA), U.S. Postal	56:51:39
2. Joseba BELOKI (Sp), ONCE	+ 4:21
3. Raimondas RUMSAS (Lit), Lampre	+ 6:39
4. Igor GONZALEZ DE GALDEANO (Sp), ONCE	+ 8:36
5. Francisco MANCEBO (Sp), IBANESTO.COM	+ 10:49
Green Jersey Robbie McEWEN (Aus), Lotto	229 pts
Polka-dot Jersey Laurent JALABERT (F), CSC-Tiscali	167 pts
White Jersey Ivan BASSO (I), Fassa	57:05:35
Team Classiification ONCE	170:56:59
Most aggressive rider Laurent JALABERT (F), CSC-Tiscali	88 pts

MADE IN COLUMBIA

Heads in the Tour for Botero, who wins his second stage victory. Tails for Christophe Moreau, forced to abandon after a fall.

The 226.5-km fifteenth stage started at 10:38 a.m. There were 163 riders in the race.

Quick start to the longest stage

In spite of the prospect of 226.5 km of racing, in the longest stage of the 89th Tour, the pace in first hour was fast (48.3 kph average). Some of the early escape attempts included Baguet and Botero. The peloton quickly chased them down by the 50 km mark. At 60 km, Botero, Aerts, and Sörensen attacked. At the first summit, the trio led the peloton by 32 seconds. In the descent, a seven-man breakaway formed (Botero, Aerts, Merckx, Magnien, Casar, Garcia-Acosta, and Hvastija). The leading seven were up by 2:50 at 83 km. Moreau abandoned after being involved in a crash before the sprint. At 87 km, the seven led by 4 minutes. The average for the second hour was 43.3 kph. At the feedzone (97.5 km) the peloton was 6:15 behind the seven-man escape.

Five passes in a row

At the top of the Col de Grimone, the gap between the escapees and the peloton was 8:45. At the fourth summit (Col du Banchet), the peloton was 10:30 behind. Their advantage dwindled to 8:40 at the top of the sixth climb (Col d'Ornon).

Botero wins his second stage

On the descent of the Col d'Ornon, Azevedo attacked the peloton. At the site of the second sprint, he was 9:05 behind the leading seven, and the peloton followed at 9:30. With 20 km to go the peloton caught Azevedo. At this stage, the pack was led by U.S. Postal, 9 minutes behind the leading seven. Jalabert was dropped on the road out of Bourg d'Oisans. Five ONCE riders dominated the peloton's chase. With 8.5 km to go, Botero launched an attack after Merckx and Aerts. Botero held on to win the stage 1:51 ahead of Aerts, who passed Merckx with about 3 km to race. Botero's average speed was 38.252 kph. Merckx claimed third (at 2:30). Heras attacked the yellow jersey's group (which included three ONCE riders—Beloki, Gonzalez de Galdeano, and Azevedo) with about 1.2 km to go.

Beloki tried, but...

At the finish, an attack by Beloki caught Heras. Armstrong followed the ONCE leader across the line in ninth place (both finishing 6:41 behind the stage winner). Lance Armstrong kept his 4:21 lead on Joseba Beloki (there were no changes to any of the other leaders' classifications).

STAGE 15 RESULTS	
1. Santiago BOTERO (Col), Kelme	**5:55:16**
2. Mario AERTS (B), Lotto	+ 1:51
3. Axel MERCKX (B), Domo	+ 2:30
4. Emmanuel MAGNIEN (F), Bonjour	+ 4:22
5. Sandy CASAR (F), FDJeux.com	+ 4:28
Green Jersey Mario AERTS (B), Lotto	25 pts
Polka-dot Jersey Axel MERCKX (B), Domo	92 pts
White Jersey Sandy CASAR (F), FDJeux.com	5:59:44
Team Classification KELME	18:02:00
Most Aggressive Rider Mario AERTS (B), Lotto	15 pts

GENERAL CLASSIFICATION	
1. Lance ARMSTRONG (USA), U.S. Postal	**62:53:36**
2. Joseba BELOKI (Sp), ONCE	+ 4:21
3. Raimondas RUMSAS (Lit), Lampre	+ 6:39
4. Igor GONZALEZ DE GALDEANO (Sp), ONCE	+ 8:50
5. Francisco MANCEBO (Sp), iBanesto.com	+ 10:44
Green Jersey Robbie McEWEN (Aus), Lotto	229 pts
Polka-dot Jersey Laurent JALABERT (F), CSC-Tiscali	173 pts
White Jersey Ivan BASSO (I), Fassa	63:07:43
Team Classification ONCE	189:03:18
Most Aggressive Rider Laurent JALABERT (F), CSC-Tiscali	88 pts

THEN BOOGERD SURGED

Since his victory in Aix-les-Bains in 1996, we've been waiting for a confirmation of Boogerd's talent.

The 179.5-km sixteenth stage began at 11:45 a.m. There were 162 riders at the sign-on. The first attack came from Bruseghin 5 km from the Galibier summit. A chase group formed (Azevedo, Nozal, Pradera, Sevilla, Botero, Jalabert, Boogerd, Blanco, and Osa). Within the last kilometer, Botero caught and passed Bruseghin. On the descent, Mazzoleni caught the nine escapees. Boogerd attacked and led the peloton by 20 seconds at the top of the Col du Télégraphe.

O'Grady attacked on the descent to gain points

On the second descent, O'Grady attacked with Turpin. He caught and passed Boogerd. At the 62 km mark, O'Grady led Boogerd, Fagnini, and Hunter by 13 seconds, Gutierrez, Merckx, Turpin, and Mayo by 22 seconds, and the peloton by 35 seconds. With 100 km to go O'Grady, Boogerd, Hunter, and Fagnini led a group of eight (Jalabert, Mayo, Gutierrez, Merckx, Turpin, Dierckxsens, Serrano, and Martinez) by 50 seconds and the peloton by 3:40. O'Grady won the first sprint. Jalabert's group was behind by 1:40. The peloton was 7:10 behind.

Col de la Madeleine

Boogerd rode away from the three other stage leaders as soon as the second climb began. When the peloton arrived, the first casualty was Sevilla (who abandoned the Tour). Mayo was the first to get clear of the attacking Jalabert group with 12 km yet to climb. With 10 km to go, Boogerd led Mayo, then Jalabert and Turpin (who caught the group of O'Grady, Hunter, and Fagnini). When Boogerd had 6 km to climb, the peloton was behind by 9 minutes. Martinez joined Jalabert's group with 75 km to race. O'Grady didn't give up on the climb, he quickly rejoined Jalabert's group on the descent. At the top, the classifications were: 1. Boogerd; 2. Jalabert at 3:20; 3. Martinez; 4. Mayo; 5. Turpin; 6. O'Grady at 3:35. Halgand led the peloton over the Col de la Madeleine.

Boogerd wins the day!

When Boogerd had 20 km to race, Boogerd led the six-man chase group by 5 minutes and the peloton by 7:15. With 12 km to climb, Boogerd led by: 5 minutes from Mayo; 5:45 from Sastre; 5:50 from Turpin; 5:55 from Merckx. The yellow jersey's peloton was 6 minutes behind the stage leader. With 7 km to go, Boogerd led Sastre by 3:54 and Armstrong, Rubiera, Heras, Leipheimer, Moncoutie, Beloki, Azevedo, Basso, Rumsas, Mancebo, and Botero by 4:48. Rubiera led the yellow jersey peloton until about the 6.5 km mark. Then Heras came to the front and dropped Botero. Lance followed his right-hand man for about 1 km before attacking. He caught Sastre 2 km from the finish. They raced together for the closing kilometers. Boogerd held on to his lead to win this demanding stage.

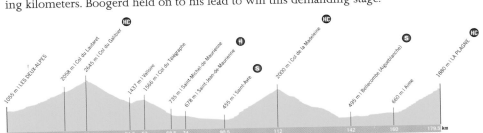

STAGE 16 RESULTS

1. Michaël BOOGERD (NI), Rabobank	5:48:29
2. Carlos SASTRE (Sp), CSC-Tiscali	+ 1:25
3. Lance ARMSTRONG (USA), U.S. Postal	+ 1:25
4. Joseba BELOKI (Sp), ONCE	+ 2:02
5. Raimondas RUMSAS (Lit), Lampre	+ 2:02

Green Jersey Michaël BOOGERD (NI), Rabobank	26 pts
Polka-dot Jersey Michaël BOOGERD (NI), Rabobank	102 pts
White Jersey Ivan BASSO (I), Fassa	5:50:43
Team Classification ONCE	17:34:22
Most Aggressive Rider Michaël BOOGERD (NI), Rabobank	25 pts

GENERAL CLASSIFICATION

1. Lance ARMSTRONG (USA), U.S. Postal	68:43:22
2. Joseba BELOKI (Sp), ONCE	+ 5:06
3. Raimondas RUMSAS (Lit), Lampre	+ 7:24
4. José AZEVEDO (P), ONCE	+ 12:08
5. Igor GONZALEZ DE GALDEANO (Sp), ONCE	+ 12:12

Green Jersey Robbie McEWEN (Aus), Lotto	229 pts
Polka-dot Jersey Laurent JALABERT (F), CSC-Tiscali	238 pts
White Jersey Ivan BASSO (I), Fassa	68:58:26
Team Classification ONCE	206:37:40
Most Aggressive Rider Laurent JALABERT (F), CSC-Tiscali	97 pts

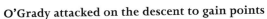

1055 m | LES DEUX-ALPES · 2058 m | Col du Lautaret · 2645 m | Col du Galibier · 1437 m | Valloire · 1566 m | Col du Télégraphe · 735 m | Saint-Michel-de-Maurienne · 678 m | Saint-Jean-de-Maurienne · 455 m | Saint-Avre · 2000 m | Col de la Madeleine · 495 m | Bellecombe (Aiguebланche) · 660 m | Aime · 1880 m | LA PLAGNE

0   25   34   51.5   57   68.5   74   90.5   112   142   160   178.5 km

AN ITALIAN REDEMPTION

By winning the sprint in Cluses, Super-Dario eliminates Super-Mario and consoles the Italian public, who wouldn't have withstood a Tour without a transalpine victory.

The 142-km seventeenth stage began at 1:02 p.m. There were 156 riders at the start: the riders who didn't take the start today were Casper, Sevilla, and Dufaux (who abandoned the Tour during stage 16); Bruylands, Rodriguez, and Oriol (outside time limit).

Aldag instigates first escape before the Col de Roselend

On the first climb a lead group of five riders formed. At the summit, the mountain points were won by Aerts, Frigo, Gutierrez, Laiseka, Guerini, Konecny. The pack was 1:15 behind. On the descent, Jalabert attacked … again! This time he was joined by Casar and Hushovd. Nozal joined them at the 50 km mark and they were 53 seconds behind the five stage leaders. At the 51.5 km mark, Laiseka, Gutierrez, Frigo, Aerts, and Guerini lead Jalabert's group by 45 seconds and a chase of eight riders by 1:25. The peloton was behind by 2:25.

Col des Saisies

With 15 km to climb to the second summit, Laiseka, Gutierrez, Frigo, Aerts, and Guerini led four (Jalabert, Jaksche, Hushovd, and Casar) by 50 seconds. Then came a group of thirteen at 1:40. The peloton was behind by 3:35. With 6 km to climb, Frigo attacked (taking Guerini and Aerts with him). With 5 km to climb, the situation was: Guerini, Frigo, and Aerts leading Gutierrez by 40 seconds; Laiseka by 1:10; Jaksche, Jalabert, Casar, and Hushovd by 2:20; Sastre by 2:35; Moncoutie, Nozal, Osa, Blanco, Serrano, Baguet, Chavanel, Bruseghin, Mazzoleni, and Lefèvre by 3 minutes and the yellow jersey's peloton by 3:45. At the feedzone, the three leaders were 3:15 ahead of a group of thirteen (Jalabert, Sastre, Jaksche, Nozal, Serrano, Gutierrez, Moncoutie, Hushovd, Casar, Osa, Baguet, Laiseka, and Lefèvre) and 5:50 ahead of the peloton. Jalabert dropped out of his group. At the sprint, the gap between the leading group and the peloton was 7:50.

A rapid victory for Frigo!

With 25 km to go, Frigo-Guerini-Aerts led nine (Moncoutie, Sastre, Jaksche, Lefèvre, Serrano, Osa, Nozal, Hushovd, and Gutierrez) by 4:05. Botero was at 6:00. The peloton was at 6:50. At the top of the fourth climb, the escapees had a 3:40 advantage on the counter-attackers, and 5:20 on the yellow jersey peloton (Armstrong, Heras, Rubiera, Beloki, Azevedo, Gonzalez de Galdeano, Basso, Kivilev, Hamilton, Leipheimer, Mancebo, Rumsas, and Goubert). The leading trio continued to work together until 2 km to go when Guerini tried several attacks without success. Aerts led out the final sprint; Frigo came around him on the right-hand side to win his first Tour stage.

STAGE 17 RESULTS	
1. Dario FRIGO (I), Tacconi	4:02:27
2. Mario AERTS (B), Lotto	s.t.
3. Giuseppe GUERINI (I), Telekom	+ 0:02
4. David MONCOUTIÉ (F), Cofidis	+ 2:55
5. Thor HUSHOVD (Nor), Crédit Agricole	+ 2:58
Green Jersey Dario FRIGO (I), Tacconi	26 pts
Polka-dot Jersey Mario AERTS (B), Lotto	110 pts
White Jersey Thor HUSHOVD (Nor), Crédit Agricole	4:05:25
Team Classification ONCE	12:17:53
Most Aggressive Rider Mario AERTS (B), Lotto	16 pts

GENERAL CLASSIFICATION	
1. Lance ARMSTRONG (USA), U.S. Postal	72:50:25
2. Joseba BELOKI (Sp), ONCE	+ 5:06
3. Raimondas RUMSAS (Lit), Lampre	+ 7:24
4. Santiago BOTERO (Col), Kelme	+ 10:59
5. José AZEVEDO (P), ONCE	+ 12:08
Green Jersey Robbie McEWEN (Aus), Lotto	229 pts
Polka-dot Jersey Laurent JALABERT (F), CSC-Tiscali	262 pts
White Jersey Ivan BASSO (I), Fassa	73:05:29
Team Classification ONCE	218:55:33
Most Aggressive Rider Laurent JALABERT (F), CSC-Tiscali	98 pts

LOOKING FOR CLUSES

Hushovd would have been wrong to give up after the cramps of the second stage: he provides Roger Legeay with a present, at the end of a difficult Tour for the Crédit Agricole team.

The 176.5-km eighteenth stage began at 12:27 p.m. with 153 riders in the race. At the 4 km mark, Van Bon attacked the peloton. He was joined at the front of the stage 1 km later by nine riders. They were Fagnini, Jaksche, Piil, Sörensen, Hushovd, Loda, Mengin, Dekker, and Loder. As the peloton passed the 20 km mark, they were 3:00 behind the ten. Lotto led the chase. Until the 65 km mark, the Lotto, U.S. Postal, and Bonjour teams kept the ten-man break in check. Near the town of Mons, however, the impetus was gone from the chase and the Van Bon group pushed their lead to 7 minutes. Jaksche was the first rider to attack. His surge took Fagnini, Sörensen, Mengin, and Loder with him. The situation with 20 km to go was: Jaksche, Mengin, and Sörensen were 10 seconds ahead of Dekker, Van Bon, Loder, Hushovd, Piil, and Fagnini and 1:10 ahead of Loda. The peloton was at 10:33. With 10 km to go: Hushovd, Mengin, and Piil led the six remnants of the escape by 39 seconds. This is how it stayed up to the final kilometer. With about 250 m to go, Piil tried to jump from behind the other two riders, but he pulled his foot from the pedal. Hushovd then bolted forward to deliver Norway its second stage success (following Lauritzen's win in 1987).

STAGE 18 RESULTS

1. Thor HUSHOVD (Nor), Crédit Agricole	4:28:28
2. Christophe MENGIN (F), FDJeux.com	s.t.
3. Jakob PIIL (Dk), CSC-Tiscali	+ 0:05
4. Leon VAN BON (Nl), Domo	+ 0:33
5. Jörg JAKSCHE (G), ONCE	+ 0:33

Green Jersey Thor HUSHOVD (Nor), Crédit Agricole	25 pts
Polka-dot Jersey Jakob PIIL (Dk), CSC-Tiscali	41 pts
White Jersey Thor HUSHOVD (Nor), Crédit Agricole	4:28:28
Team Classification CSC-TISCALI	13:37:44
Most Aggressive Rider Leon VAN BON (Nl), Domo	13 pts

GENERAL CLASSIFICATION

1. Lance ARMSTRONG (USA), U.S. Postal	77:30:35
2. Joseba BELOKI (Sp), ONCE	+ 5:06
3. Raimondas RUMSAS (Lit), Lampre	+ 7:24
4. Santiago BOTERO (Col), Kelme	+ 10:59
5. José AZEVEDO (P), ONCE	+ 12:08

Green Jersey Robbie McEWEN (Aus), Lotto	239 pts
Polka-dot Jersey Laurent JALABERT (F), CSC-Tiscali	262 pts
White Jersey Ivan BASSO (I), Fassa	77:45:39
Team Classification ONCE	232:44:54
Most Aggressive Rider Laurent JALABERT (F), CSC-Tiscali	98 pts

ARMSTRONG SO STRONG

With his talent at its highest level, Lance Armstrong spells it out: he is the boss!

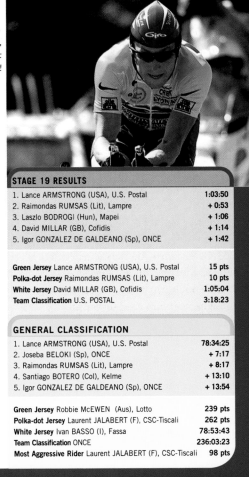

There were two headlines from the nineteenth stage. The first was that Lance Armstrong won his fifteenth Tour stage. The second story was about Raimondas Rumsas and how equipment failure cost him dearly. Yes, Lance was superb. He won this time trial just as he planned. His 47 kph average shattered the efforts of the Colombian, Santiago Botero, who beat him in the 52-km time trial of stage 9. Lance proved that he's the boss of the bunch and that he can cope with the pressure of being the race leader and the defending champion. He could spin a cadence of about 110 rpm and not even need to rise from the saddle on a steep climb. But all of this might have not have happened were it not for Rumsas's faulty handlebars. Over the rise, Rumsas had a lead of 17 seconds on Lance. By the time he arrived at the 33 km split, he had dropped behind by 7 seconds. The Lithuanian wrestled his bike with such vigor that the bolts on his bars loosened. And he rode the final 40 km with a damaged bike—and without the ability to pull on his bars for fear that they might move more and cause a fall. At the finish his second place was 1 minute better than Joseba Beloki—the rider who will stand next to Lance in second place in Paris. That's life. That's cycling. . . .

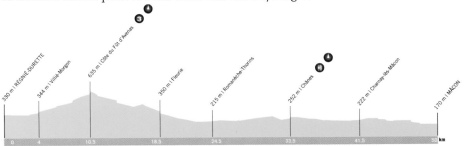

STAGE 19 RESULTS

1. Lance ARMSTRONG (USA), U.S. Postal	1:03:50
2. Raimondas RUMSAS (Lit), Lampre	+ 0:53
3. Laszlo BODROGI (Hun), Mapei	+ 1:06
4. David MILLAR (GB), Cofidis	+ 1:14
5. Igor GONZALEZ DE GALDEANO (Sp), ONCE	+ 1:42

Green Jersey Lance ARMSTRONG (USA), U.S. Postal	15 pts
Polka-dot Jersey Raimondas RUMSAS (Lit), Lampre	10 pts
White Jersey David MILLAR (GB), Cofidis	1:05:04
Team Classification U.S. POSTAL	3:18:23

GENERAL CLASSIFICATION

1. Lance ARMSTRONG (USA), U.S. Postal	78:34:25
2. Joseba BELOKI (Sp), ONCE	+ 7:17
3. Raimondas RUMSAS (Lit), Lampre	+ 8:17
4. Santiago BOTERO (Col), Kelme	+ 13:10
5. Igor GONZALEZ DE GALDEANO (Sp), ONCE	+ 13:54

Green Jersey Robbie McEWEN (Aus), Lotto	239 pts
Polka-dot Jersey Laurent JALABERT (F), CSC-Tiscali	262 pts
White Jersey Ivan BASSO (I), Fassa	78:53:43
Team Classification ONCE	236:03:23
Most Aggressive Rider Laurent JALABERT (F), CSC-Tiscali	98 pts

A kangaroo bounds along on the Champs-Elysées and beats another Australian, Baden Cooke.

AN AUSTRALIAN IN GREEN

The final stage of the 2002 Tour de France began at 1:41 p.m. There were 153 riders still in the race. The main feature of the stage was the quest to determine a leader of the green jersey classification. McEwen led Zabel 239 points to 238 points at the start of the stage.

McEwen adds two more points to his lead

The peloton was content to roll along (at an average speed of just 30.2 kph in the first hour). The festivities of this parade stage took a back seat 3 km from the site of the first sprint. Telekom led the peloton to the sprint, but McEwen surged about 350 m from the line and took 6 points. The peloton was led into Paris by the U.S. Postal team. On the approach to the Champs-Élysées, Jalabert was the first to attack. He was quickly chased down. Zabel and McEwen were not near the front for the second sprint.

Attacking action

Some of the riders in the early laps of the Champs-Élysées were: Mattan, Vasseur, Piil, Morin, Loda, De Groot, Flickinger, and Hvastija. With 8 laps to race, Moreni, and Chavanel attacked. Near the Arc de Triomphe, Chavanel punctured. Moreni continued. He was then chased down by Jalabert, Millar, Tafi, and his teammate Radealli. With 5 laps to go, the chase group caught Jalabert's group. Rumsas was in the chase group which held a maximum lead of 37 seconds when ONCE came to the front of the peloton. With 4 laps to go, Rumsas dropped out of the escape group. Nine riders (Piil, Velo, Dekker, Wauters, Horrillo, Zubeldia, Brognara, Moreni, and Halgand) were 10 seconds ahead of the peloton with 3 laps to go. They worked up a maximum lead of 25 seconds. With 2 laps to go the nine led by 15 seconds. The escape was over with 9 km to go.

McEwen wins the sprint and the best sprinter's jersey!

As usual, the last Tour stage was a sprinter's story. Australian Baden Cooke led the sprint out, but was caught by a rapid McEwen with about 50 m to go. The Lotto rider's win secured his victory over Erik Zabel in the green jersey classification (280 points to 261). Lance Armstrong's fourth successive Tour title was won with an average speed of 39.919 kph (the fourth-fastest in history).

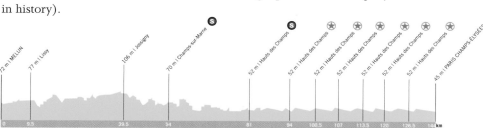

STAGE 20 RESULTS

1. Robbie McEWEN (Aus), Lotto		3:30:47
2. Baden COOKE (Aus), FDJeux.com		s.t.
3. Damien NAZON (F), Bonjour		s.t.
4. Fabien BALDATO (I), Fassa		s.t.
5. Davide CASAROTTO (I), Alessio		s.t.

Green Jersey Robbie McEWEN (Aus), Lotto	41 pts
White Jersey Baden COOKE (Aus), FDJeux.com	3:30:47
Team Classification FASSA	10:32:21
Most Aggressive Rider Christian MORENI (I), Alessio	11 pts

GENERAL CLASSIFICATION

1. Lance ARMSTRONG (USA), U.S. Postal	82:05:12
2. Joseba BELOKI (Sp), ONCE	+ 7:17
3. Raimondas RUMSAS (Lit), Lampre	+ 8:17
4. Santiago BOTERO (Col), Kelme	+ 13:10
5. Igor GONZALEZ DE GALDEANO (Sp), ONCE	+ 13:54

Green Jersey Robbie McEWEN (Aus), Lotto	280 pts
Polka-dot Jersey Laurent JALABERT (F), CSC-Tiscali	262 pts
White Jersey Ivan BASSO (I), Fassa	82:24:30
Team Classification ONCE	246:36:14
Most Aggressive Rider Laurent JALABERT (F), CSC-Tiscali	100 pts

Results

General classification (YELLOW JERSEY)

1	ARMSTRONG Lance	USA	U.S. Postal	82:05:12	50	AERTS Mario	B	Lotto	+ 1:31:17
2	BELOKI Joseba	Sp	ONCE	+ 07:17	51	NIERMANN Grischa	G	Rabobank	+ 1:33:03
3	RUMSAS Raimondas	Lit	Lampre	+ 08:17	52	HALGAND Patrice	F	Delatour	+ 1:35:38
4	BOTERO Santiago	Col	Kelme	+ 13:10	53	PERON Andrea	I	CSC-Tiscali	+ 1:39:42
5	GONZALEZ de GALDEANO Igor	Sp	ONCE	+ 13:54	54	VELO Marco	I	Fassa	+ 1:39:46
6	AZEVEDO José	P	ONCE	+ 15:44	55	VASSEUR Cédric	F	Cofidis	+ 1:40:52
7	MANCEBO Francisco	Sp	iBanesto.com	+ 16:05	56	LIVINGSTON Kevin	USA	Telekom	+ 1:44:51
8	LEIPHEIMER Levy	USA	Rabobank	+ 17:11	57	BLANCO Santiago	Sp	iBanesto.com	+ 1:45:09
9	HERAS Roberto	Sp	U.S. Postal	+ 17:12	58	EKIMOV Viatcheslav	Rus	U.S. Postal	+ 1:45:51
10	SASTRE Carlos	Sp	CSC-Tiscali	+ 19:05	59	HINCAPIE George	USA	U.S. Postal	+ 1:47:35
11	BASSO Ivan	I	Fassa	+ 19:18	60	ETXEBARRIA David	Sp	Euskaltel	+ 1:48:19
12	BOOGERD Michaël	NI	Rabobank	+ 20:33	61	LANDIS Floyd	USA	U.S. Postal	+ 1:48:31
13	MONCOUTIÉ David	F	Cofidis	+ 21:08	62	BODROGI Laszlo	Hun	Mapei	+ 1:50:05
14	LELLI Massimiliano	I	Cofidis	+ 27:51	63	TRAMPUSCH Gerhard	A	Mapei	+ 1:51:30
15	HAMILTON Tyler	USA	CSC-Tiscali	+ 28:36	64	HONCHAR Serhiy	Ukr	Fassa	+ 1:52:59
16	VIRENQUE Richard	F	Domo	+ 28:42	65	KONECNY Tomas	Cz	Domo	+ 1:53:26
17	GOUBERT Stéphane	F	Delatour	+ 29:51	66	MORENI Cristian	I	Alessio	+ 1:54:17
18	OSA Unaï	Sp	iBanesto.com	+ 30:17	67	BESSY Frédéric	F	Crédit Agricole	+ 1:58:58
19	VOGONDY Nicolas	F	FDJeux.com	+ 32:44	68	MILLAR David	GB	Cofidis	+ 1:59:51
20	SÖRENSEN Nicki	Dk	CSC-Tiscali	+ 32:56	69	PADRNOS Pavel	Cz	U.S. Postal	+ 2:03:10
21	KIVILEV Andreï	Kaz	Cofidis	+ 33:41	70	MAZZOLENI Eddy	I	Tacconi	+ 2:03:46
22	RUBIERA José Luis	Sp	U.S. Postal	+ 36:43	71	TURPIN Ludovic	F	AG2R	+ 2:04:50
23	GOTTI Ivan	I	Alessio	+ 40:16	72	ALDAG Rolf	G	Telekom	+ 2:04:56
24	BARANOWSKI Dariusz	Pl	iBanesto.com	+ 43:04	73	PEÑA Victor Hugo	Col	U.S. Postal	+ 2:05:24
25	FRIGO Dario	I	Tacconi	+ 43:15	74	SERPELLINI Marco	I	Lampre	+ 2:05:55
26	BROCHARD Laurent	F	Delatour	+ 44:02	75	BORTOLAMI Gianluca	I	Tacconi	+ 2:06:57
27	ZBERG Beat	Swi	Rabobank	+ 44:29	76	PRADERA Mikel	Sp	ONCE	+ 2:07:00
28	MERCKX Axel	B	Domo	+ 45:39	77	O'GRADY Stuart	Aus	Crédit Agricole	+ 2:07:02
29	GUTIERREZ José Enrique	Sp	Kelme	+ 50:59	78	OLANO Abraham	Sp	ONCE	+ 2:08:25
30	BOTCHAROV Alexandre	Rus	AG2R	+ 51:52	79	FERNANDEZ Bingen	Sp	Cofidis	+ 2:08:29
31	JAKSCHE Jörg	G	ONCE	+ 56:05	80	GUERINI Giuseppe	I	Telekom	+ 2:09:26
32	ROBIN Jean-Cyril	F	FDJeux.com	+ 57:35	81	IVANOV Sergueï	Rus	Fassa	+ 2:10:07
33	SERRANO Marcos	Sp	ONCE	+ 1:00:52	82	ZABEL Erik	G	Telekom	+ 2:10:33
34	LEFÈVRE Laurent	F	Delatour	+ 1:07:00	83	CASAR Sandy	F	FDJeux.com	+ 2:12:22
35	BRANDT Christophe	B	Lotto	+ 1:07:50	84	LATASA David	Sp	iBanesto.com	+ 2:13:01
36	CHAVANEL Sylvain	F	Bonjour	+ 1:09:26	85	RENIER Franck	F	Bonjour	+ 2:15:08
37	JULICH Bobby	USA	Telekom	+ 1:13:11	86	MENGIN Christophe	F	FDJeux.com	+ 2:16:47
38	NOZAL Isidro	Sp	ONCE	+ 1:13:27	87	PINEAU Jérôme	F	Bonjour	+ 2:18:24
39	ZUBELDIA Haimar	Sp	Euskaltel	+ 1:15:39	88	MAYO Iban	Sp	Euskaltel	+ 2:18:27
40	GUSTOV Volodomir	Ukr	Fassa	+ 1:17:26	89	JOACHIM Benoît	Lux	U.S. Postal	+ 2:19:27
41	CHAURREAU Iñigo	Sp	AG2R	+ 1:17:37	90	MORIN Anthony	F	Crédit Agricole	+ 2:19:55
42	JALABERT Laurent	F	CSC-Tiscali	+ 1:17:48	91	WAUTERS Marc	B	Rabobank	+ 2:20:30
43	WADECKI Piotr	Pl	Domo	+ 1:18:12	92	MIKHAÏLOV Guennadi	Rus	Lotto	+ 2:20:39
44	MARTINEZ Miguel	F	Mapei	+ 1:18:42	93	MENCHOV Denis	Rus	iBanesto.com	+ 2:21:31
45	BELLI Wladimir	I	Fassa	+ 1:19:41	94	ENGELS Addy	NI	Rabobank	+ 2:21:37
46	LAISEKA Roberto	Sp	Euskaltel	+ 1:20:08	95	PASCUAL Javier	Sp	iBanesto.com	+ 2:22:11
47	BRUSEGHIN Marzio	I	iBanesto.com	+ 1:26:57	96	MAGNIEN Emmanuel	F	Bonjour	+ 2:22:39
48	BÖLTS Udo	G	Telekom	+ 1:29:32	97	HUNTER Robert	SA	Mapei	+ 2:25:32
49	CUESTA Inigo	Sp	Cofidis	+ 1:29:59	98	LODER Thierry	F	AG2R	+ 2:25:35

99 WESEMANN Steffen	G	Telekom	+ 2:30:21
100 EDALEINE Christophe	F	Delatour	+ 2:31:03
101 FAGNINI Gian Matteo	I	Telekom	+ 2:32:00
102 BERNARD Jérôme	F	Delatour	+ 2:32:19
103 FLICKINGER Andy	F	AG2R	+ 2:33:13
104 HONDO Danilo	G	Telekom	+ 2:34:21
105 BAGUET Serge	B	Lotto	+ 2:34:24
106 TAFI Andrea	I	Mapei	+ 2:34:34
107 HORILLO Pedro	Sp	Mapei	+ 2:35:32
108 DIERCKXSENS Ludo	B	Lampre	+ 2:38:44
109 McGEE Bradley	Aus	FDJeux.com	+ 2:39:02
110 VOIGT Jens	G	Crédit Agricole	+ 2:39:35
111 CABELLO Francisco	Sp	Kelme	+ 2:40:13
112 HUSHOVD Thor	Nor	Crédit Agricole	+ 2:40:43
113 DESSEL Cyril	F	Delatour	+ 2:41:24
114 BOUYER Franck	F	Bonjour	+ 2:41:42
115 AUGÉ Stéphane	F	Delatour	+ 2:43:14
116 ZABALLA Constantino	Sp	Kelme	+ 2:44:30
117 BÉNÉTEAU Walter	F	Bonjour	+ 2:45:15
118 BELOHVOSCIKS Raivis	Lat	Lampre	+ 2:46:30
119 BROGNARA Andrea	I	Alessio	+ 2:47:10
120 VAN HYFTE Paul	B	CSC-Tiscali	+ 2:49:20
121 LODA Nicola	I	Fassa	+ 2:49:22
122 GARCIA ACOSTA Vicente	Sp	iBanesto.com	+ 2:52:44
123 MATTAN Nico	B	Cofidis	+ 2:55:10
124 CASSANI Enrico	I	Domo	+ 2:55:24
125 PIIL Jakob	Dk	CSC-Tiscali	+ 2:55:32
126 MARICHAL Thierry	B	Lotto	+ 3:00:01
127 COOKE Baden	Aus	FDJeux.com	+ 3:00:22
128 HVASTIJA Martin	Slo	Alessio	+ 3:00:38
129 VAN BON Leon	NI	Domo	+ 3:02:46
130 McEWEN Robbie	Aus	Lotto	+ 3:03:30
131 SVORADA Jan	Slo	Lampre	+ 3:03:30
132 BALDATO Fabio	I	Fassa	+ 3:04:07
133 DE GROOT Bram	NI	Rabobank	+ 3:04:44
134 VIDAL José Angel	Sp	Kelme	+ 3:06:37
135 RADAELLI Mauro	I	Tacconi	+ 3:06:43
136 DEKKER Erik	NI	Rabobank	+ 3:07:56
137 KNAVEN Servais	NI	Domo	+ 3:09:57
138 BERTOGLIATI Rubens	Swi	Lampre	+ 3:10:10
139 APOLLONIO Massimo	I	Tacconi	+ 3:10:11
140 CORTINOVIS Alessandro	I	Lampre	+ 3:11:10
141 ETXEBARRIA Unaï	Ven	Euskaltel	+ 3:11:18
142 ARRIZABALAGA Gorka	Sp	Euskaltel	+ 3:12:45
143 SEIGNEUR Eddy	F	Delatour	+ 3:12:49
144 AGNOLUTTO Christophe	F	AG2R	+ 3:13:15
145 DE CLERCQ Hans	B	Lotto	+ 3:14:14
146 KROON Karsten	NI	Rabobank	+ 3:14:51
147 HINAULT Sébastien	F	Crédit Agricole	+ 3:15:10
148 LANGELLA Anthony	F	Crédit Agricole	+ 3:16:54
149 CASAROTTO Davide	I	Alessio	+ 3:16:56
150 BERGÈS Stéphane	F	AG2R	+ 3:20:44
151 NAZON Damien	F	Bonjour	+ 3:22:25
152 PIZIKS Arvis	Lit	CSC-Tiscali	+ 3:34:57
153 FLORES Igor	Sp	Euskaltel	+ 3:35:52

Points classification
(GREEN JERSEY)

1 McEWEN Robbie	Aus	Lotto	280 pts
2 ZABEL Erik	G	Telekom	261 pts
3 O'GRADY Stuart	Aus	Crédit Agricole	208 pts
4 COOKE Baden	Aus	FDJeux.com	198 pts
5 SVORADA Jan	Slo	Lampre	154 pts

Best Climber classification
(POLKA-DOT JERSEY)

1 JALABERT Laurent	F	CSC-Tiscali	262 pts
2 AERTS Mario	B	Lotto	178 pts
3 BOTERO Santiago	Col	Kelme	162 pts
4 ARMSTRONG Lance	USA	U.S. Postal	159 pts
5 MERCKX Axel	B	Domo	121 pts

Best Young Rider classification
(WHITE JERSEY)

1 BASSO Ivan	I	Fassa	82:24:30
2 VOGONDY Nicolas	F	FDJeux.com	+ 13:26
3 BRANDT Christophe	B	Lotto	+ 48:32
4 CHAVANEL Sylvain	F	Bonjour	+ 50:08
5 NOZAL Isidro	Sp	ONCE	+ 54:09

Team classification

1 ONCE - EROSKI	246:36:14
2 U.S. POSTAL SERVICE	+ 22:49
3 TEAM CSC-TISCALI	+ 30:17
4 iBANESTO.COM	+ 34:06
5 COFIDIS CRÉDIT PAR TÉLÉPHONE	+ 36:19
6 RABOBANK	+ 40:41
7 JEAN DELATOUR	+ 1:17:21
8 KELME - COSTA BLANCA	+ 1:42:22
9 DOMO—FARM FRITES	+ 1:46:20
10 FASSA BORTOLO	+ 2:01:59
11 FDJEUX.COM	+ 2:40:14
12 AG2R PRÉVOYANCE	+ 2:58:25
13 TEAM TELEKOM	+ 3:04:59
14 EUSKALTEL - EUSKADI	+ 3:15:23
15 ALESSIO	+ 3:20:07
16 MAPEI - QUICK STEP	+ 3:47:35
17 CRÉDIT AGRICOLE	+ 3:52:50
18 BONJOUR	+ 3:55:50
19 LOTTO - ADECCO	+ 3:57:12
20 LAMPRE - DAIKIN	+ 4:01:41
21 TACCONI SPORT	+ 4:07:24

Most Aggressive Rider
(RED BIB)

1 JALABERT Laurent	F	CSC-Tiscali	100 pts
2 RENIER Franck	F	Bonjour	50 pts
3 HUSHOVD Thor	Nor	Crédit Agricole	35 pts
4 BOOGERD Michaël	NI	Rabobank	33 pts
5 DIERCKXSENS Ludo	B	Lampre	33 pts

THE PHOTO GALLERY

TOUR DE FRANCE VIPS

All Tour de France VIPs emphasize how welcome they feel and this is largely attributed to the kindness and availability of the race personalities. An overall feeling of joy and elation conveys to the visitors a full appreciation of the event's magnitude. Orson Welles described the Tour de France as a "Hollywood superproduction," after being present in the front row (in Jacques Goddet's car) in 1950. During the 1920s, Douglas Fairbanks followed several stages on a motorcycle. More recently, Dustin Hoffman came to the Tour to greet Greg LeMond. This year, it was Robin Williams who arrived on the Tour scene via parachute to encourage his friend Lance Armstrong. He was filled with enthusiasm, "The Ventoux, it's Disneyland," he declared in the *Village Départ*.

AMERICANS IN THE PELOTON

Lance Armstrong's recent Tour victories might lead us to forget that the command of American cycling cannot be reduced to the strength of just one man. On the contrary, this year's Tour de France's peloton included nine highly talented American riders. On the U.S. Postal Service Team, two compatriots were Lance's body-and-bike guards: the up-and-coming rider Floyd Landis, riding his first Tour ever, and veteran George Hincapie, riding his seventh. They carried out their duties so well and helped their leader with such devotion that they were complimented by the Boss himself as the "best team ever!" Three compatriots and former U.S. Postal team members were also participating in the event: Levy Leipheimer (Rabobank), who finished eighth in the race, showed great talent and could even challenge the four-time winner in 2003; Tyler Hamilton (CSC-Tiscali), who had great fun with Laurent Jalabert during the medical check-up, finished fifteenth; and Kevin Livingston, who seems a subdued racer since moving to Telekom in 2001. His team-mate Bobby Julich, who came in third in the 1998 Tour, placed thirty-seventh overall this year. Finally, Fred Rodriguez (Domo–Farm Frites), who gave up during stage 16, still had time enough to show his red and blue helmet, whereas the unlucky Jonathan Vaughters (Crédit Agricole) was forced to abandon during stage 11. The final count—9 Americans in a peloton of 189 riders—amounts to 5 percent of the pack. Together the American riders staged an outstanding performance in the Tour.

GENERATIONS

Like all passions, the "Tour fever," an
indescribable desire to participate in
the July celebration, is transmitted from
generation to generation and often its
signs can be seen early on, as illustrated
in this picture of a very young supporter
of Lance Armstrong. Everywhere on the
roadsides of Luxembourg, Germany, and
France, one can see many babies,
toddlers, and small children cheering
with their families. Their support and joy
brings encouragement to the riders in
the peloton, who connect with a young
public. The older generation also has a
strong presence at the Tour. In the space
of four days the race visited Quincampoix
and St. Méen-le-Grand, the villages
where the late French Tour legends
Jacques Anquetil and Louison Bobet are
respectively laid to rest. In St. Méen-
le-Grand, the race followed the Rue
Louison Bobet and passed in front of the
museum devoted to the Brittany champion. Former Tour riders Jean Bobet and
Francis Pipelin, both from St. Méen, were
present along with Pierre Barbotin,
Louison's most faithful teammate.
Spanning generations, the Tour draws all
of us in.

THE AMERICAN INVASION

When reporters in Sallanches, where the French five-time Tour winner Bernard Hinault became world champion, asked Lance Armstrong whether he had noticed more Americans lining the roadsides of the Tour de France, he answered, "Progressively, each year, I see more American supporters. They are also more numerous at the finish in Paris, a destination highly appreciated by my compatriots. On the Champs-Elysées, there are also quite a few people from Austin, and more and more Texas flags." Indeed, at the finish line, Lance's American supporters held a victory party and celebrated his success. All along the route fans cheered Armstrong and his team on to victory—one enthusiast wore a U.S. soccer team uniform and ran alongside the yellow jersey waving a big Texas flag, a Tour first. Armstrong's ongoing success introduces a new era to the Tour.

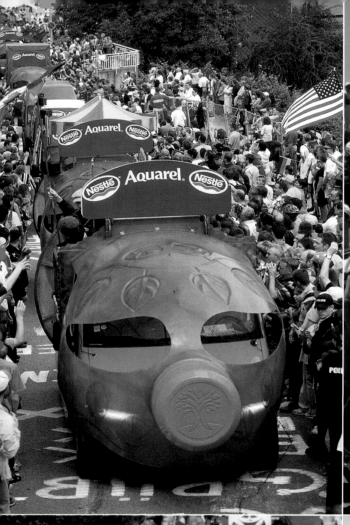

THE OTHER SPECTACLE

Since 1930, the publicity caravan has been a pillar of the Tour de France and a source of ongoing pleasure for the public. Some twelve million promotional items are distributed every year and contribute greatly to the success of the operation. The procession of brightly colored vehicles are long awaited, particularly when, like Nestlé Aquarel, they distribute cold water to thirsty spectators who spend long hours in the sun. As Hubert Genieys, director of public relations for the Nestlé Waters Group, says so well: "In our role as partner, we would like to contribute actively to the success of the Tour. This competition, soon to be one hundred years old, is endowed with a formidable expertise, on logistic and sports levels; but the caravan, symbolic of the Tour's festive dimension, still offers many possibilities for brand names. It is a virgin territory where many things remain to be accomplished." See you in 2003!

THE VILLAGE

Before the start of each stage, the Tour de France followers, a community of some three thousand people, meet up in the Tour de France Village, a restricted area that constitutes the heart of the race for three hours every morning. Here it is possible to have coffee, meet the riders, get a haircut, negotiate an interview with Tour directors Jean-Marie Leblanc or Patrice Clerc, read the daily press, or even chat with former great champions like the Three Musketeers—Raymond Poulidor, Jean Stablinski, and Henry Anglade. Poulidor wore the Crédit Lyonnais yellow jersey for three weeks and signed a record number of autographs. Stablinski, public relations attaché for Astra, presented former regional road racers every morning in the departure village. As for Anglade, he was in charge of the Relais-Étape, the Grande Boucle's authentic traveling expo. This enabled him to meet up with his former race companions, in particular his friend Hubert Ferrer. There's always something going on in the Village!

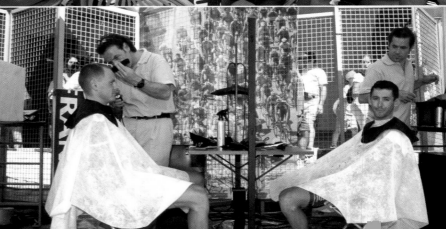

MAIRIE DE PAR

TOUR DE LANCE!

Since his first Tour win in 1999, Lance Armstrong has become the most famous American cyclist, and his four consecutive victories in the Tour de France have made him an American hero. He recovered from testicular cancer in 1996, and made a spectacular athletic comeback in 1998. His story is so amazing that his personal achievements have elevated him beyond the world of sports, as his friendship with President George W. Bush testifies. More than a champion, Lance Armstrong is a symbol of strength and stamina for his American public. Notwithstanding his celebrity status, the champion from Texas has remained a modest man, who knows from personal experience that life can deal you both the best and the worst. When he visited the charred ruins of World Trade Center in Manhattan last September, he spoke simple but powerful words, expressing distress about the attacks and compassion for the victims, while at the same time giving solace to the victim's families and survivors. In July at Reims, Armstrong hosted a family who lost their father, a NYC fireman, in the tragic collapse of the twin towers (pictured below). On a less tragic note, he also welcomed his good friend, actor Robin Williams, to this year's Tour (pictured right). On his ride on the Champs-Elysées, he was cheered on by a contingency of U.S. and Texas fans, all celebrating a victorious American in Paris.

ARRIED BY THE CROWD

obbie McEwen, who dethroned Erik Zabel
the points classification, and Ivan Basso,
e best young rider in this 2002 Tour, must
ave been impressed by the dense crowds
ning the roadside to watch the peloton
ass by. The Tour is known to be popular,
ut this year's throngs were totally unex-
ected! The growing crowds didn't trouble
e cool Australian, who succeeded where
s compatriot Stuart O'Grady failed last
ear. From the start of the season, the
ustralian champion has competed with
ghtning legs, taking more than a dozen
ctories. Even during massage sessions,
e PMU green jersey is not out of his sight.
it fatherhood that has given McEwen such
ability and an unwavering focus for the
print? Or is he simply gifted with pure tal-
nt that he had never exploited up until
ow? Pure talent was evident in the overall
erformance of Ivan Basso, who was award-
d the white jersey for the best young rider
the competition. The young Italian had to
ght hard to win against the Scotsman
avid Millar—dare we say his new white
ersey suits him well?

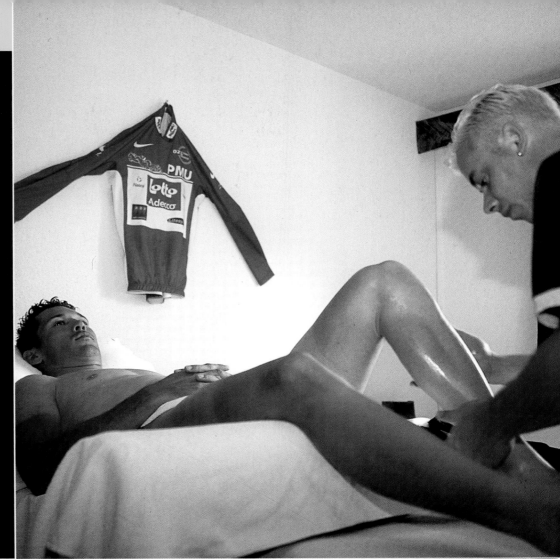

ALT: 721M
M^T VENTOUX 14
11,1% SUR 1Km

UT OF THE ORDINARY

mong these unusual pictures that tell their
wn story, we remember the wonderful adven-
re of Michel Bationo, the Tour of Burkina
aso chalkboard official recruited in West
rica by the Tour de France organizers to do
e same job at the Tour de France. The strap-
ng thirty-six-year-old, who dislikes heat and
un, is a teacher of physical education at the
cal Bambata secondary school in Ouaga-
ougou (locally known as "Ouaga"), is mar-
ed and father of an eight-year-old daughter,
nd has been a UCI national commissaire
nce 1996. Michel was noticed by Jean-
arie Leblanc when the ASO company took
ver the promotion of the Tour of Burkina Faso
October 2001. A dream came true in July
efore the eyes of thousands of television
ectators who, moved by the smile of this
iendly chalkboarder on the television
creen, took to Bationo right away. An anec-
ote better illustrates the character: Laurent
alabert, on a solitary breakaway on a moun-
in stage, addressed him by his first name to
sk him to swap his motorcycle for his bike.
e reply: "Mister Jalabert, life is a choice!
ome on, be brave, keep going, my Gallic
ousin." The joie de vivre and the sincerity of
e Burkina Faso inhabitants, the country of
right men, is definitely not a myth.

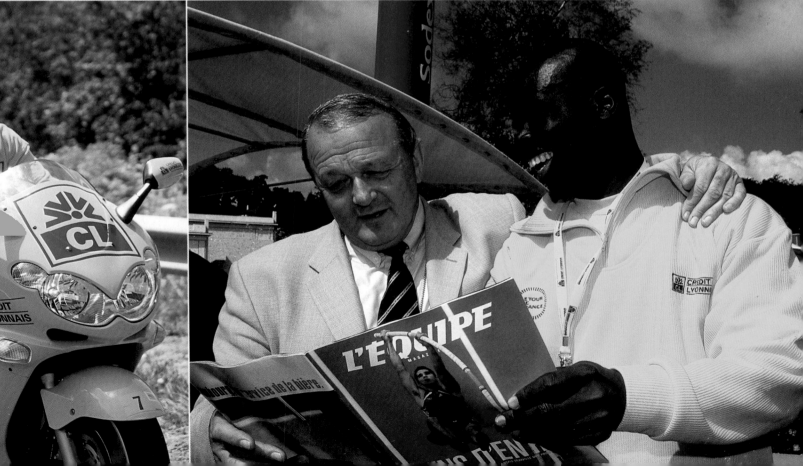

Armstrong's Fourth Consecutive Victory

Change within continuity. This expression could be used to sum up the 2002 Tour. The fourth consecutive triumph for Lance Armstrong is obviously similar to his previous ones: he used the same method, the same strategy, we can even say the same determination. It is different from the other years in that the American champion and his principal opponents were confronted with new situations. Cycling as a competition is in a continual state of evolution and transformation. In spite of appearances, the 2002 Tour de France had original and unexpected moments. It wasn't a repeat of the 2001 Tour, as there were numerous alterations to the script.

Certainly, Lance Armstrong forged his success from the beginning by knocking out an anxious opposition in the prologue and, like last year, consolidating his position through the following time trial stages of which he is the master. Otherwise, he raced efficiently, without trying to create large gaps (for what purpose?) and without taking refuge in a overly stereotypical attitude. Over the last four years, the favorite of the Tour hasn't changed his habits. From experience, he endeavors to keep his challengers at a distance and to protect himself with a reasonable margin of safety—approximately six to seven minutes. This is reflected in his advance on each immediate rival over the years: 7:37 in 1999 (over Alex Zülle), 6:02 in 2000 (over Jan Ullrich), 6:44 in 2001 (over Ullrich), and 7:17 in 2002 (over Joseba Beloki).

But his fourth victory was the most impressive, perhaps the greatest. It allowed him to precede Louison Bobet and Greg LeMond in the record books, a performance that speaks for itself. He also follows hot on the heels of record holders Jacques Anquetil, Eddy Merckx, Bernard Hinault, and Miguel Induráin, whose five consecutive wins he intends to equal in 2003, the Centennial edition of the competition. It is difficult to imagine that Armstrong will stop when he is doing so well, and the experts believe he is capable of six consecutive victories, a feat that has never been achieved.

The 2002 Tour marks the apotheosis of Armstrong's art of mastery and skill. Armstrong is not only better equipped, athletically and organically; he is also the most ambitious, methodical, conscientious, and motivated competitor. Tied to an exceptional determination, equal, if not superior to that of Bobet, Anquetil, Merckx, and Induráin, who were models of will power, he incorporates that little "extra" with regard to his opponents in all areas of the race: a courage cemented by the discipline of year-round training, a unique sense of organization, and a formidable zeal in his work. In short, a hyper-professionalism. He also possesses an aptitude for extreme climates, an important asset. Formerly presented as the man of the cold and the rain, he is equally adept in extreme heat. His resting heart rate (32 beats per minute) adapts itself to the greatest workloads, an enormous advantage in the mountains. With his physical qualities he is a natural elite climber, and his high-cadence pedaling technique proved to be the perfect style for climbing passes smoothly with maximum efficiency.

This 30-year-old from Texas, with his conquest of Europe road racing and the Tour de France, decidedly knows all there is to know about cycling. He is at one and the same time an old hand who trains according to both the principles of Antonin Magne and yet a novice who anticipates every strategic move. His success is most logical, as surely as failure would have been a profound injustice.

It must never be forgotten that before winning the Tour de France, Armstrong won the fight against cancer. His exploits today extend beyond the sport of cycling to communicate immense hope to millions of cancer-stricken men and women.

Who would have won the Tour in the absence of Armstrong?

The U.S. Postal Service team champion has widened his athletic influence with a humanitarian crusade, giving his support to medical research. Our respect for him is great—his detractors are discredited and those who insulted him on the Ventoux should be ashamed.

The question has been asked: Who would have won the Tour in the absence of Armstrong? The runner up, Beloki? It's not certain. Botero, Rumsas, Gonzalez

de Galdeano, or an unknown outsider? But, above all, who would really have merited this honor? The inventory confirms this observation: The four-time winner didn't have a rival to match him and his superiority was all the more crushing with a powerful team within which Roberto Heras and José Luis Rubiera played outstanding roles.

In spite of the flagrant domination of the man in the yellow jersey, this hot, fast Tour de France of long breakaways was an exciting one. It gave rise to a compelling and attractive race, if at times frenzied. During the first hour of a stage it was common for the riders to cover nearly fifty kilometers, and several times the average speed was more than 46 kph. Patrice Halgand, in brilliant form, won one of the fastest stages in history in Pau. Richard Virenque won back his supporters, and Laurent Jalabert, the spectators' favorite, transformed his last Tour de France into a triumphal parade. However, the strong personalities of the two darlings of the French public should not allow us to forget the name of the top French finisher, David Moncoutié. The Australian McEwen put an end to Zabel's long reign by winning the green jersey in convincing fashion (a fitting example of the international flavor of cycling). David Millar, winner in Béziers, revealed a new angle to his talent; Axel Merckx, tenth in 1998, made a remarkable reappearance; and Thor Hushovd, the Norwegian from the Crédit Agricole team, deprived Christophe Mengin of a stage victory in Bourg-en-Bresse. Finally, the new French wave of riders—Sylvain Chavanel, Nicolas Vogondy, Sandy Casar, Franck Renier, Stéphane Bergès, Christophe Edaleine, Miguel Martinez (the mountain bike renegade), and Jérôme Pineau (the youngest rider in the Tour)—produced some nice surprises. Laurent Brochard, Jean-Cyril Robin, Laurent Lefèvre the Northerner, and Stéphane Goubert the Southerner fully justified their selection. In short, a wonderful Tour.

Acknowledgments

The Official Tour de France Annual is published
by Amaury Sport Organisation:
2 Rue Rouget-de-Lisle
F-92130 Issy-les-Moulineaux
Telephone: 00 33 (0)1 41 33 15 00
Fax: 00 33 (0)1 41 33 15 09

A.S.O.: Patrice Clerc, President
Christian Duxin, Jean-Marie Leblanc, Gilbert Ysern, General Managing Directors

Texts: Jean-Marie Leblanc, Jacques Augendre & Denis Descamps

Translation: Theresa O'Neill & Denis Descamps

Editor: Zarko Telebak

Copyediting: Jill Redding and John Wilcockson

Photographers: Bruno Bade, Ingrid Hoffmann and Jean-Christophe Moreau
Motorbike drivers: Jean-Pierre Levenbrück, Jean-Pierre Fiumelli and Serge Seynaeve
Picture Library: Didier Blondel, Pascal Perrève, Thibaut L'Hopital and Thibaud Serre

Special thanks to Catherine Gitton and Marie-Laure Denoeud
for their invaluable collaboration and their unfailing support.

Thank you also to Christian Boulnois, who drove Jacques Augendre
in a masterly fashion on the sunny roads of the Tour de France.

Thank you lastly to Yann Le Moënner, Director of the A.S.O. Media Department, to Philippe Sudres,
Director of the Press Service, to Christophe Marchadier, to Sandrine Guinot and to all the members
of the Tour de France Press Service (Nicolas Cazeneuve, Adrien Brandon, Darren Horspool, Marie Leblanc,
Michaële Cernela and Patrick Janning), who accompanied us in this thrilling adventure, the 2002 Tour de France.

Printed in Spain

International Standard Book Number: 1-931382-11-5

Library of Congress Cataloging-in-Publication Data applied for.

VeloPress®
1830 North 55th Street
Boulder, Colorado 80301–2700
303/440-0601; Fax 303-444-6788; E-mail velopress@7dogs.com